AUTHOR
DICK MILLS   KU-656-924

ILLUSTRATORS
JOAN THOMPSON
PHILIP WEARE

DESIGNED AND EDITED
BY
ERIC INGLEFIELD

CONSULTANT
DR. DAVID FORD

CONTENTS

INTRODUCTION

What Are Aquarium Fishes?

Some years ago, the answer to the question 'What are aquarium fishes?' would have been one word: Goldfish. That single fish, *Carassius auratus*, paved the way for today's hobby, which now embraces fishes from all over the world. Coldwater and tropical freshwater species make up the majority of fishes kept in the aquarium and garden pools, but there is a growing number of aquarists keeping tropical marine fishes from the coral reefs of the Indo–Pacific oceans. It is also possible to keep fishes which can tolerate both fresh and salt water; these are found in brackish waters in estuaries and coastal waters.

How It All Began

Originally, fishes were kept for their food value, in moats and ponds, but gradually (particularly in China) it became the practice to keep the more highly coloured fishes for their beauty alone. The first recorded instance of a coloured Carp was in AD 970. The Goldfish was introduced into Europe in the 17th century and within a few years its popularity had become established. Some two hundred years were to pass before the first tropical species was brought from China, not only to be kept, but also bred in the aquarium. The fish was the Paradise Fish, *Macropodus opercularis*, which is still enjoying popularity today (see page 81).

The first tropical aquarium was a very primitive affair, with gas and oil lamps being used to maintain the water's necessary warmth. From the 1920s onwards there was a huge upsurge of interest in fishkeeping; magazines devoted to the subject flourished, as did Aquarium Societies. Following the two World Wars, the impetus resumed, and modern air transport now brings constant supplies of fishes for our aquaria in a matter of hours, instead of days or weeks.

ALAN CALLENDER
6 DETLING HSE
CONGREVE ST
WALWORTH
SE 17

AQUARIUM FISHES

WARD LOCK

A KINGFISHER BOOK
First published in Great Britain in 1980
by Ward Lock Limited, 116 Baker Street, London W1M 2BB,
a Pentos company

Designed and produced by Grisewood & Dempsey Ltd
Grosvenor House, 141-143 Drury Lane, London WC2B 5TG
© Kingfisher Books Limited 1980

Colour separations by Newsele Litho Ltd, Milan, London
Printed and bound by Vallardi Industrie Grafiche, Milan

Mills, Dick
    Aquarium fishes.—(Kingfisher guides).
    1. Aquariums
    I. Title II. Series
    639'.34   SF457

    ISBN 0-7063-5943-7

ACKNOWLEDGEMENTS
The author and publishers wish to thank the following for their help in supplying photographs for
this book on the pages indicated :

Heather Angel cover, 41, 69, 76, 89 ; Bruce Coleman 19, 33, 38, 53, 54 (Jane Burton) ; 23 (Hans
Reinhard) ; 43 (S. C. Bisserot) ; 118 (Bill Wood) ; Natural Science Photos/L. E. Perkins 8, 15 ;
Keith Sagar 4, 6, 111 ; SeaPhot/Peter Scoones 104 ; Ian Sellick 84. Picture research by Penny
Warn.

Maps by Tony Mould. Additional artwork by Hayward Art Group.

FURTHER INFORMATION
For further information about fishkeeping or help with your aquarium problems, write to our
consultant : Dr D. M. Ford ; Animal Studies Centre ; Freeby Lane ; Waltham-on-the-Wolds ;
Melton Mowbray ; Leicestershire ; LE14 4RT.

Behaviour and Habits of Fishes

There are aquarium fishes to fit almost any imaginable shape and colour, and their behaviour and habits are equally diverse. Body shapes may be disc- or torpedo-shaped; movements may be graceful or constantly rapid. Some fishes are nocturnal, whilst others are happy to be seen at any time, even taking food from the hobbyist's fingers. Many species will breed in the aquarium and, here again, there are many methods of breeding procedures for the aquarist to learn about and enjoy.

Physical Characteristics

Whatever final shape a fish attains in adulthood, it retains certain basic physical characteristics, although these may be modified to suit the fish's local environment.

The *fins* may be paired, or single, and are used for locomotion and stability. The small, non-functioning *adipose fin* is not always present. The anal fin of male livebearing fishes is modified into a *gonopodium*, the reproductive organ (see page 69). The *mouth* is situated to suit the fish's feeding habits – upturned for surface feeders, underslung for bottom and algae feeders. The *barbels* are taste-sensitive, whisker-like growths around the mouths of some fishes, and are particularly highly developed in bottom-dwelling fishes such as Catfishes (pages 55-62). The *gills* are the fish's respiratory organs, extracting dissolved oxygen from the water, although some fishes have auxillary organs which allow them to breathe atmospheric air if necessary. The *lateral line* is a sensory system; vibrations in the water are detected through a row of openings along the flanks of the fish which are connected to nerve endings.

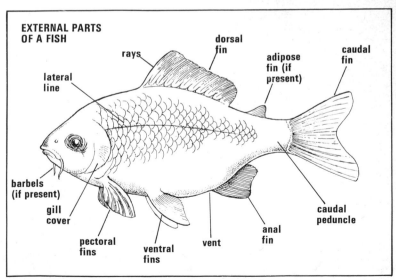

EXTERNAL PARTS OF A FISH

rays — dorsal fin — adipose fin (if present) — caudal fin — lateral line — barbels (if present) — gill cover — pectoral fins — ventral fins — vent — anal fin — caudal peduncle

Aquarium Equipment

The Tank Tanks may either be of all-glass construction or have metal frames. Because of the corrosive effect of salt water, however, metal-framed tanks and metal reflector hoods should not be used for marine aquaria. A tank hood of some kind should always be used, however, on all aquaria, because it not only houses the aquarium lighting and cuts down evaporation losses, but also prevents fishes from escaping.

Heating A heating system is essential for the tropical aquarium and today's electric heaters and thermostats are entirely reliable. Large tanks (1 metre (3 ft) long and over) may require the use of two heaters to provide an even spread of heat. Thermostats, which may be of an internal (submersible) or external (non-submersible) type, are usually set at the factory to operate at around 24°C (75°F) but have provision for adjustment by the aquarist. Combined heater and thermostat units are also available. The water temperature is checked by means of an aquarium thermometer of either the floating or adhesive type.

Lighting Either tungsten lighting (bulbs) or fluorescent tubes may be used, or a combination of both. Some experimentation may be necessary to arrive at the correct amount and intensity of light for satisfactory plant growth without any unwanted growth of algae (usually caused by too much light, or too few aquatic plants). It is usual practice to illuminate the aquarium to suit the aquarist, say, 10-12 hours a day.

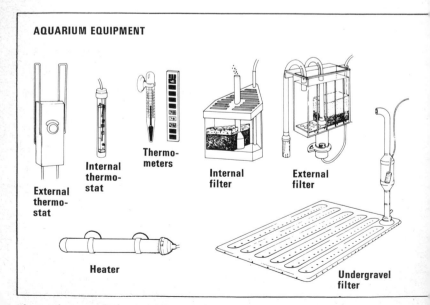

AQUARIUM EQUIPMENT

External thermostat

Internal thermostat

Thermometers

Internal filter

External filter

Heater

Undergravel filter

Aeration and Filtration Aeration is often wrongly regarded as obligatory in the aquarium, but a small electric vibrator air-pump can also provide enough air to operate a *filter*, which removes suspended matter from the water, together with some of the unwanted dissolved minerals. Filters can be installed either inside or outside the tank, and the larger models may be electrically driven. A different form of filtration is provided by the biological, undergravel type (installed in the tank before the gravel); this type of filter is essential in marine aquaria and its operation is discussed elsewhere in this Guide (page 15).

Water Most freshwater fishes may be kept in water from the domestic supply, even though its hardness may vary from one part of the country to another. Certain species of fishes, such as the Characins, do seem to thrive better in soft water, whilst the Livebearing Fishes and most African Cichlids prefer much harder water. Many aquarists also take heed of the water's acidity and alkalinity, but this need not concern the newcomer to the hobby unduly as most fishes are hardy enough to acclimatize themselves to whatever conditions exist in the aquarium. Fishes needing more specialized water conditions are best left alone until the basic rudiments of fishkeeping have been mastered with the hardier (and less expensive) species. Marine fishes require salt water, and although this may be collected (from an unpolluted source) by aquarists living near the sea, it is more usual for synthetic seawater to be used, made from proprietary brands of aquarium seawater salt mixes.

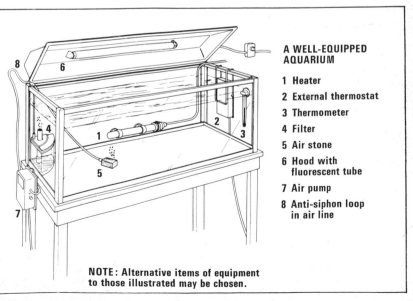

A WELL-EQUIPPED AQUARIUM

1 Heater
2 External thermostat
3 Thermometer
4 Filter
5 Air stone
6 Hood with fluorescent tube
7 Air pump
8 Anti-siphon loop in air line

NOTE: Alternative items of equipment to those illustrated may be chosen.

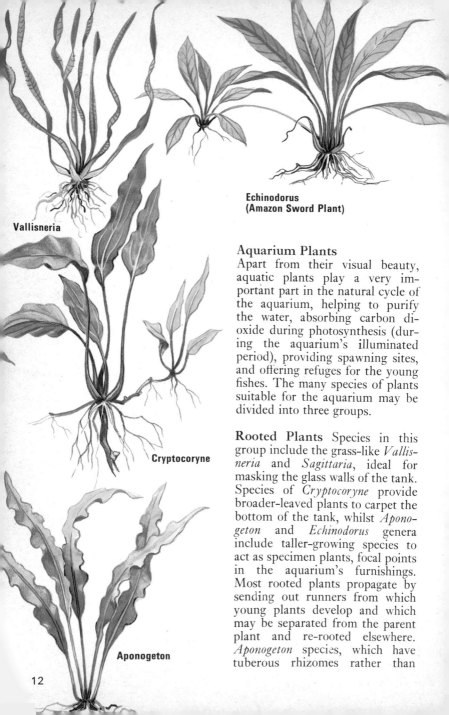

**Echinodorus
(Amazon Sword Plant)**

Vallisneria

Cryptocoryne

Aponogeton

Aquarium Plants

Apart from their visual beauty, aquatic plants play a very important part in the natural cycle of the aquarium, helping to purify the water, absorbing carbon dioxide during photosynthesis (during the aquarium's illuminated period), providing spawning sites, and offering refuges for the young fishes. The many species of plants suitable for the aquarium may be divided into three groups.

Rooted Plants Species in this group include the grass-like *Vallisneria* and *Sagittaria*, ideal for masking the glass walls of the tank. Species of *Cryptocoryne* provide broader-leaved plants to carpet the bottom of the tank, whilst *Aponogeton* and *Echinodorus* genera include taller-growing species to act as specimen plants, focal points in the aquarium's furnishings. Most rooted plants propagate by sending out runners from which young plants develop and which may be separated from the parent plant and re-rooted elsewhere. *Aponogeton* species, which have tuberous rhizomes rather than

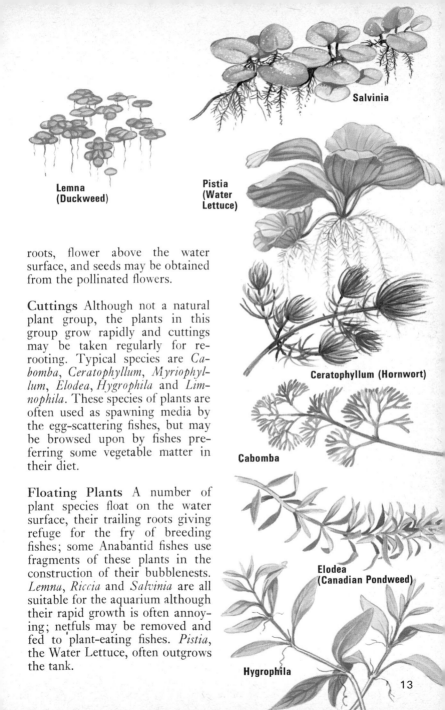

Salvinia

Lemna
(Duckweed)

Pistia
(Water
Lettuce)

Ceratophyllum (Hornwort)

Cabomba

Elodea
(Canadian Pondweed)

Hygrophila

roots, flower above the water surface, and seeds may be obtained from the pollinated flowers.

Cuttings Although not a natural plant group, the plants in this group grow rapidly and cuttings may be taken regularly for re-rooting. Typical species are *Cabomba*, *Ceratophyllum*, *Myriophyllum*, *Elodea*, *Hygrophila* and *Limnophila*. These species of plants are often used as spawning media by the egg-scattering fishes, but may be browsed upon by fishes preferring some vegetable matter in their diet.

Floating Plants A number of plant species float on the water surface, their trailing roots giving refuge for the fry of breeding fishes; some Anabantid fishes use fragments of these plants in the construction of their bubblenests. *Lemna*, *Riccia* and *Salvinia* are all suitable for the aquarium although their rapid growth is often annoying; netfuls may be removed and fed to plant-eating fishes. *Pistia*, the Water Lettuce, often outgrows the tank.

13

Setting up the Freshwater Aquarium

The aquarium gravel (washed before use) should be deep enough to allow aquatic plants to root satisfactorily, and is often banked up from front to back to allow the plants to grow undisturbed around the walls of the tank whilst allowing the fishes adequate swimming space near the front – where the aquarist can see them. After arranging the gravel in its desired contours, rocks can be set in place; large rocks should be set directly on the aquarium base to prevent toppling. The heating system is now installed (if needed), as is the filtration system.

When filling the tank, the water should be poured into a cup or saucer standing on the gravel; the overflow will fill the tank without disturbing the contours of the gravel. The tank, when about two-thirds full, may be planted and then topped up. The heating and lighting is then switched on and the filtration system started. Before adding the fishes, the aquarium should be operated for at least two weeks while the plants become established.

A basic tank layout. The large rocks disguise the corners, whilst the placing of tall plants behind bushier species gives an illusion of distance.

A side view shows how the gravel is sloped upward from front to back.

Setting up the Marine Aquarium

The first thing to be placed in the tank is the undergravel filter, followed by a layer of coral sand or synthetic substitute at least 50 mm (2 in) deep. Pieces of coral, and other tank decorations, can now be arranged as desired. Heaters and the thermostat are also fitted at this time, but no metal clips (unless stainless steel) or rubber suction pads should be used as they will quickly corrode in the salt water. Where an outside thermostat is used, the wire securing-clip should be covered with a length of plastic air-line before being fitted into place.

The marine tank can either be brightly lit (as in the fishes' native coral reef), or more subdued lighting may be used. The former results

When compared to the freshwater aquarium, the marine tank at first seems bare due to the lack of plants, but this 'loss' is soon made up by the inclusion of such invertebrates as Sea-anemones, Starfishes and Tubeworms. The aquarium does not only benefit visually: for example, Clownfishes make their homes among the tentacles of the Sea-anemones. Just as fascinating is the chance to grow living Coral in the marine aquarium.

in a growth of algae over the coral and rocks (more welcome here than in the freshwater tank), bringing a hint of greenery and providing food for some fishes. As yet, there are few species of marine plants that thrive in the aquarium. The more dimly-lit aquarium will not be so affected by algal growth, but the colours of the corals and other tank decorations will be seen more clearly.

The salt water, unless collected from a clean, natural source, should be mixed according to the manufacturer's instructions, and the specific gravity reading taken. It is usual for this figure to lie somewhere between 1.020 and 1.025, and readings are taken by means of an inexpensive aquarium hydrometer.

After filling the tank, the heating, lighting and filtration systems should be switched on and the tank left to mature. This initial period is to allow a bacteria colony to develop in the aquarium bed and this is sustained by the flow of oxygen-carrying water drawn through the sand by the undergravel filter system. The function of these bacteria is to break down toxic nitrogenous compounds into less harmful substances; the level of the toxic substances (nitrites) can be measured by an inexpensive nitrite testing kit. The air supply to the undergravel filter should NEVER BE SWITCHED OFF for any length of time, otherwise the bacteria colony will die, resulting in a massive pollution of the aquarium.

It is not until the nitrite level has fallen to a safe level that fishes and other sea creatures can be introduced into the aquarium. In addition to the work done by the bacteria in keeping toxic levels to a minimum, the partial water changes carried out by the aquarist also achieve a similar result. It is possible to equip the marine aquarium with other, highly sophisticated filtration and sterilization devices, but these are beyond the scope of this Guide.

Stocking the Aquarium

An aquarium's fish-holding capacity depends on the amount of water surface area available, and not on the volume of water contained. A formula allowing a certain area of water surface for a given length of fish is a safer guide than the old principle of 'so many inches of fish per gallon of water'. A rough indication is set out in the table below.

A new fish is introduced to its new home with as little shock as possible.

> *Tropical fishes (freshwater):* 75 sq cm (12 sq in) of surface area per 2.5 cm (1 in) body length
> *Coldwater fishes (freshwater):* 190 sq cm (30 sq in) per 2.5 cm (1 in) body length
> *Tropical fishes (marine):* 300 sq cm (48 sq in) per 2.5 cm (1 in) body length

In addition to this purely physical size/space ratio there are other factors to consider, such as the fishes' natural swimming habits and general sociability. By studying the fishes' physical features and characteristics outlined in this Guide it will be possible to choose a selection of fishes to occupy all levels of the tank and which should get on well together.

When faced with the actual choice of fishes at the aquatic supplier, select healthy stock. A healthy fish should hold its fins erect and appear to be full of life; avoid fishes that are hollow-bellied, have folded fins (unless this is a natural characteristic) and which hide and sulk in the corner of the tank. Likewise, any fish with physical deformities, obvious wounds, spots or pimples should not be considered a worthwhile investment. If the intended choice is one of the more exotic species or a marine fish, ask if it is feeding regularly (slightly different from being fed regularly), and if it is being kept in any special water conditions, which may differ from your own domestic supply. Checking the specific gravity of the water to which the fishes are accustomed is also advised in the case of marine fishes.

Fishes should be introduced into the aquarium with as little shock as possible. They should be floated (still in their plastic transportation bag) in the aquarium for a few minutes to equalize the water temperatures; some aquarists also introduce some aquarium water into the plastic bag during this period to acclimatize the fish to its quality. Only after this process has taken place can the fishes be gently released into their new home.

Feeding

With the exception of some marine species, which may have to be educated to take unfamiliar foods, fishes are not generally fussy feeders. A wide range of commercially prepared, dried foods are available which provide all the fishes' dietary needs. In addition, live foods may be given, such as freshwater crustacea, insect larvae and chopped garden worms; other live foods may be cultured, such as Micro-worm, Grindal Worm and White Worm. The eggs of the Brine Shrimp, *Artemia salina*, may be hatched in salt water to provide a disease-free, highly nutritious live food for young fishes. Lean raw meat and fish roe are also relished, and chopped spinach, lettuce and oat flakes are welcomed by fishes preferring a vegetarian diet. Marine fishes may also be given these foods, together with the meat of shellfish.

Fishes which do not normally feed on the bottom may be fed worms from a floating feeder.

A close watch must always be kept to see that all offered food is consumed completely. Any food surplus to the fishes' immediate requirements will sink to the bottom and soon begin to pollute the tank; the rule is to feed only enough food for the fishes to consume in a few minutes.

Because nocturnal fishes may miss the daytime feedings, some food may be introduced into the aquarium late at night to cater for their needs.

Maintenance of the Aquarium

Daily checks on the fish population, temperature and specific gravity (marine aquaria only) soon become automatic, but some tasks take a little longer. The pruning of aquatic plants, the removal of dead plant leaves and detritus from the tank floor, and the cleaning and replacement of filter media are best done at weekends. Partial water changes (usually 10-20 per cent) can be made every 6-8 weeks, perhaps more frequently for marine aquaria; any water used to replace that removed should be at approximately the same temperature and of the same composition. Evaporation losses in marine aquaria are replaced with *fresh* water, as the dissolved salts are not lost from the aquarium except when water changes are made, in which case salt water of the correct specific gravity should be added.

Any growth of algae on the front glass can be removed with a scraper, but it is usual to leave growths of algae on the side and back walls of the aquarium for the fishes to browse upon.

Diseases

Quarantining of fishes can do much to prevent the introduction of disease into the aquarium, and all new additions should be kept in a separate tank for two weeks so that any signs of latent disease can easily be detected. At the end of this period the fishes may be declared fit to be introduced into the main collection. Ideally, quarantining should also include plants, and live foods from suspect aquatic sources should be avoided. Should the worst occur, the hobbyist should learn to recognize the signs of the more common ailments, for which there are effective, proprietary remedies.

White Spot (*Ichthyophthiriasis*) The fish is peppered with tiny white spots. Easily cured.

Shimmying Not a disease but a sign of chilling or shock. The temperature should be raised 1-2°C (2°F), or more if necessary.

Fin Rot Infection that sets in after physical fin damage has occurred. Easily cured in clean water with antibiotics.

Oodinium A parasitic infection of marine fishes, similar in appearance to the White Spot of freshwater aquaria, although the spots may be rust-coloured as well as grey-white. Curable with proprietary remedies based on copper.

Fungus Cotton-wool-like growths on the skin. Responds to salt water baths or malachite green/methylene blue treatment.

Mouth fungus (caused by a slime bacteria which resembles fungus) is only cured by means of antibiotics.

Lack of space prevents more detailed information on diseases and their remedies, but most aquatic manufacturers operate expert advisory services.

Breeding

Fishes reproduce by means of eggs, which are fertilized either inside or outside the female fish's body.

Egglaying Species Most fishes scatter eggs into the water, where they are fertilized by the male fish's milt. The adult fishes are likely to eat their own eggs in the aquarium, so some form of protection must be provided, such as thick bushy plants or net screens. Other species deposit the eggs on pre-selected sites or in bubblenests, and show great parental care for the eggs and fry. Some fishes are mouthbrooders: the fertilized eggs are incubated in the mouth of the female fish until hatching occurs.

Livebearing Species These fishes also produce eggs, but they develop into tiny fishes inside the female fish's body and are then released as free-swimming fry. Again, some adult fishes are not averse to eating their own young, and the *gravid* (pregnant) female should be given a thickly planted separate tank in which to give birth.

A male Siamese Fighting Fish making a nest by blowing bubbles.

Fish Classification and Sizes
All fishes are classified scientifically by a *binomial* system, a generic name followed by a specific name; thus, *Barbus oligolepis* and *Barbus titteya* are two species within the genus *Barbus*, but *Moenkhausia oligolepis* is a totally unrelated fish within the genus *Moenkhausia*, although it bears a similar specific name.

Freshwater fish sizes quoted in this Guide are those expected to be attained in aquarium-kept fishes, not necessarily those of adult fishes in the wild. Sizes for marine fishes are based upon natural proportions, but these may not necessarily be attained by fishes in captivity. The fishes illustrated are adult males, unless stated otherwise.

Additional Information
There are many Aquatic Societies throughout the world, some of which specialize in certain species of fishes; much practical information can be obtained by joining such organizations or from aquatic magazines.

FRESHWATER FISHES

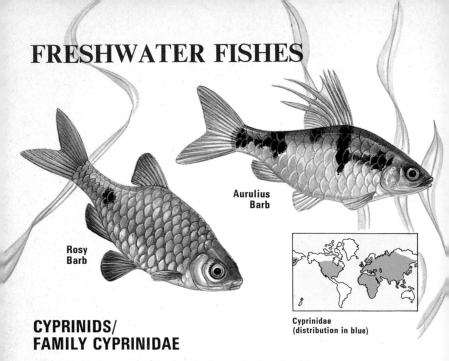

Aurulius
Barb

Rosy
Barb

Cyprinidae
(distribution in blue)

CYPRINIDS/
FAMILY CYPRINIDAE

This family has 1500 species, both tropical and coldwater. Only
Australasia, South America, Malagasy, and the Arctic regions of
Canada, Greenland and Iceland are without indigenous Cyprinid fishes.
India and the Far East are the natural homes of the Barbs, Rasboras
and Danios, whilst the Goldfish and Koi, originally cultured in China
and Japan, now occupy many ornamental lakes in other countries.

Cyprinid fishes have no teeth in the jaws, but rely on pharyngeal
teeth in the throat to break up their food. The physical arrangement
of these pharyngeal teeth plays a very important part in the
identification and classification of individual fishes in the group. The
fact that most have barbels around the mouth gives a clue to their
normal life-pattern; they tend to occupy the lower levels in the water
and are often seen rummaging around the tank gravel for food. They
are sociable, even gregarious, and feel happier (and look better too)
in shoals. Some Barbs tend to be boisterous, and a solitary specimen
amongst other fishes may develop into a fin-nipper – perhaps out of
sheer boredom.

Reproduction is by egg-scattering, fertilization occurring in the
water. Some method of 'egg-saving' is usually practised by hobbyists
to prevent the fertilized eggs being eaten by the adult fishes.

With their bright colours, hearty appetites and constant activity
it is not hard to understand the popularity of this group of fishes with
the aquarist.

BARBS

These Bream-like fishes are native to Africa and Asia. They are active, colourful fishes which are hardy, undemanding and highly suitable for the warm water aquarium.

Aurulius Barb; Longfin Barb *Barbus aurulius* 105 mm 4 in. Southeast India: still and running water. The scarlet tips to the caudal fin and the blue-green sheen to the scales above the lateral line make for a colourful fish. Two half-completed dark transverse bands with intermediate blotches adorn the flanks, and the belly may take on a pinkish hue. The chief feature is the extension of the dorsal fin into long filaments in mature males. *Temperature:* 24°C (75°F). *Diet:* live and dry foods accepted. *Breeding:* not prolific. A notorious egg-eater.

Rosy Barb *Barbus conchonius* 100 mm 4 in. Northern India, Assam, Bengal: still and running water. This well-established aquarium favourite grows larger in nature, and specimens over 125 mm (5 in) have been reported. The male's colour changes from dark bronze/green to an intense rosy-red during breeding. The fins are black. A long-finned strain has recently been introduced to the hobby, but it is a man-made variety, not a natural occurrence. *Temperature:* 24°C (75°F). *Diet:* will eat anything. *Breeding:* very prolific.

Cuming's Barb *Barbus cumingi* 50 mm 2 in. Sri Lanka: mountain and forest streams. A smart little Barb of yellow/bronze colours. Two black diamonds appear on the fish's sides, and the fins are yellow and red. Females are similar, but the males may have the more intense colour. *Temperature:* 24°C (75°F). *Diet:* live and dried foods. *Breeding:* as may be expected from its natural habitat, the addition of some cooler, fresh water to its tank may trigger off a spawning sequence. Females are more rounded-out when ripe.

Striped Barb; Zebra Barb *Barbus fasciatus* 100 mm 4 in. Malaysia: all kinds of water. A proportionately longer fish with dark horizontal lines on a golden yellow body. These lines may be incomplete in young specimens, only developing into continuous lines with maturity. Some confusion may occur between this fish and *B. lineatus,* which is almost identical. However, *B. lineatus* has no barbels. An active fish, constantly patrolling its tank, which should be large enough to accommodate several specimens. *Temperature:* 24°C (75°F). *Diet:* live and dried foods. *Breeding:* none reported as yet.

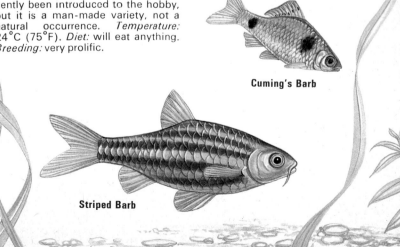

Cuming's Barb

Striped Barb

Golden Dwarf Barb *Barbus gelius* 38 mm 1½ in. Central India: slow-moving, densely vegetated waters. The smallest of the Barb family, this species appears to have gone out of favour with aquarists recently, possibly because it is not so highly coloured as its relatives. The body is suffused with a golden sheen, and there are dark patches on the flanks. The male fishes may have a reddish band running from head to tail following the lateral line. Fins may be yellowish. *Temperature:* 20°C (68°F) ; may be reduced a little during winter. *Diet:* all small foods, both live and dried. *Breeding:* possible, fry very small. Breeding temperature not to exceed 22°C (72°F).

Black Ruby Barb; Purple-headed Barb *Barbus nigrofasciatus* 65 mm 2½ in. Sri Lanka: slow-moving water. Another fish in which the male's coloration is transformed at breeding time. Normally a dull yellow-gold body with three or four dark, transverse bands and sooty-coloured fins; when in prime condition, the male turns a deep, rich ruby colour and the fins darken to jet black. The scales take on an iridescence and can show a green tinge in reflected light. Females are less colourful and do not change at breeding time. *Temperature:* 24°C (75°F). *Diet:* all foods. *Breeding:* prolific; temperature may be raised a little to induce spawning.

Checker Barb; Island Barb *Barbus oligolepis* 50 mm 2 in. Indonesia, Sumatra: all waters. This fish may be recognized instantly by its dark-edged scales, which give it a checkered appearance. A metallic, purple sheen is more obvious in the male's colouring above the lateral line, and the dorsal and anal fins of the male fish are dark-edged. The female is less colourful and tends towards a dull yellowish brown. *Temperature:* 24°C (75°F). *Diet:* all foods. *Breeding:* ready breeders.

Golden Barb *Barbus schuberti* 70 mm 2¾ in. The origins of this fish are obscure; it appears to be a man-made variety, probably from *Barbus semifasciolatus* stock (a very similar fish but of greenish-yellow hue), but another ancestor may be *Barbus sachsi*. A bright yellow fish with red fins, the males having more dark flecks on the flanks than the females, which, in their turn, may be more recognizable by their plumpness when viewed from above. Sometimes this fish suffers from 'blood-blisters' on the body and in the fins. *Temperature:* 24°C (75°F). *Diet:* all foods. *Breeding:* prolific.

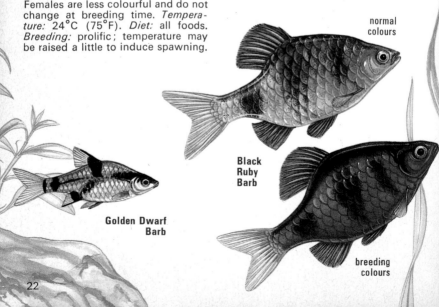

normal colours

Black Ruby Barb

Golden Dwarf Barb

breeding colours

A group of Tiger Barbs.

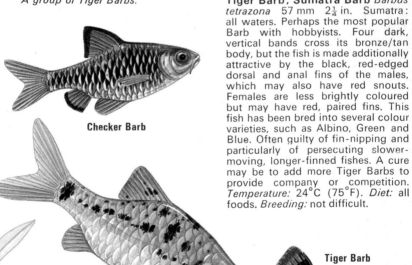

Checker Barb

Golden Barb

Tiger Barb

Tiger Barb; Sumatra Barb *Barbus tetrazona* 57 mm 2¼ in. Sumatra: all waters. Perhaps the most popular Barb with hobbyists. Four dark, vertical bands cross its bronze/tan body, but the fish is made additionally attractive by the black, red-edged dorsal and anal fins of the males, which may also have red snouts. Females are less brightly coloured but may have red, paired fins. This fish has been bred into several colour varieties, such as Albino, Green and Blue. Often guilty of fin-nipping and particularly of persecuting slower-moving, longer-finned fishes. A cure may be to add more Tiger Barbs to provide company or competition. *Temperature:* 24°C (75°F). *Diet:* all foods. *Breeding:* not difficult.

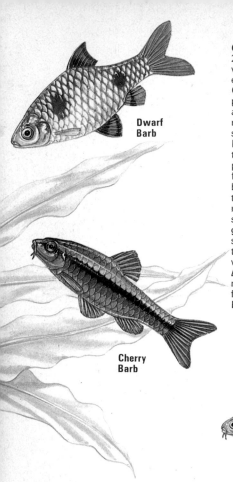

Dwarf Barb

Cherry Barb

Livebearing Barb

Cherry Barb *Barbus titteya* 50 mm 2 in. Sri Lanka: densely planted waters. Similar in size, but more elongate than the Checker Barb, the Cherry Barb has an even, speckled patterning which is more intense above the lateral line. A dark band runs from snout to caudal fin in both sexes, with a faint gold line above it. Males may have a metallic sheen to the area above the line and their predominant coloration is cherry red; females are more of a drab red-brown. The male's colours are intensified when in the presence of a ripe female, and the male often stretches and displays his fins so energetically that they may split. This species may be a little shy, and thickets of refuge-giving plants are welcomed. *Temperature:* 24°C (75°F). *Diet:* all foods, including vegetable matter such as soft algae scrapings from the tank glass. *Breeding:* usual Barb methods.

Dwarf Barb; Pygmy Barb *Barbus phutunio* 50 mm 2 in. India, Sri Lanka, Burma. Other similar fishes are the Ticto, or Two Spot, Barb (*B. ticto*), and Stoliczk's, or the Platinum, Barb (*B. stoliczkanus*). These fishes are often confused with each other and the differences are indeed small. All have red dorsals with black markings, and black markings often adorn the flanks. *B. ticto* has an incomplete lateral line, *B. stoliczkanus* a complete line. *B. phutunio* has a purple sheen to the belly region when in good condition. *Temperature:* 24°C (75°F). *Diet:* all foods. *Breeding:* all possible.

Livebearing Barb; Silver Barb *Barbus viviparus* 65 mm 2½ in. Southeast Africa: exact details of habitat unknown. This Barb was bequeathed its specific name upon the evidence of young fry being found in its body when dissected; however, these were later found to be young fry that had been eaten and not waiting to be born. A silvery fish with a distinctive black line, which divides into two for part of the way, and runs from snout to caudal fin. There is a black spot at the base of the anal fin. *Temperature:* 24°C (75°F). *Diet:* all foods. *Breeding:* no details known.

SOME LARGER BARBS

Clown Barb *Barbus everetti* 140 mm 5½ in. South-east Asia; all waters. Vertical dark bands cross the red-orange body. The fins are pink/red. A much larger fish than other vertically-banded Barbs and heavy in proportion. Females can be larger than the males, but less vividly coloured. *Temperature:* 24°C (75°F). *Diet:* all foods, including green matter (which may include the aquarium's soft-leaved plants). *Breeding:* very prolific.

Spanner Barb; 'T' Barb *Barbus lateristriga* 125 mm 5 in. Malaysia, Thailand: streams and pools. The two vertical dark bands immediately behind the gill cover, together with a dark horizontal line to the caudal fin, give the fish its common name; 'T' Barb is an American name (the 'T' is lying on its side). The fins are black, and the body shade may be soft pink/silver. *Temperature:* 24°C (75°F). *Diet:* all foods. *Breeding:* very prolific.

Tinfoil Barb; Goldfoil Barb; Schwanenfeld's Barb *Barbus schwanenfeldi* 300 mm 12 in. The largest Barb. The scales reflect like bright tin, with the scales near the dorsal surface having a golden sheen. The fins are bright red, with the caudal and dorsal being edged with black. This active fish will spend the day cruising up and down the tank eating anything that comes its way — including plants. It does not attack other fishes but may cause them some discomfort by its sheer size and turbulence as it passes. Obviously needs a large tank and may become the favourite of its owner. Plastic plants may be used to decorate the aquarium if necessary, but must be anchored down securely. Young fishes are very attractive, and are often purchased in ignorance of their likely adult size by newcomers to the hobby. *Temperature:* 24°C (75°F). *Diet:* all foods, see above. *Breeding:* has been bred in large aquaria.

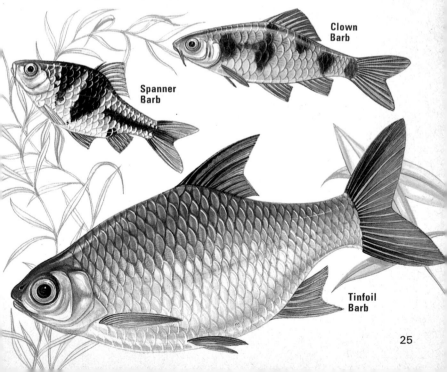

Clown Barb

Spanner Barb

Tinfoil Barb

RASBORAS

Rasboras are slender fishes that usually swim in large schools in the upper levels of tropical waters. They are undemanding and tolerant and consequently popular community fishes.

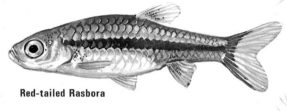

Red-tailed Rasbora

Harlequin Fish

Red-tailed Rasbora *Rasbora borapetensis* 50 mm 2 in. Thailand: still, and slow-moving waters. This slender fish is silver-coloured; a horizontal dark stripe runs from behind the gill cover to the root of the caudal fin and is accentuated by a parallel gold band above it. Another dark line follows the lower contour edge of the fish rearwards from the anal fin. The anterior part of the caudal is bright red. There appears to be little difference in visible characteristics to enable reliable sex distinction to be made. The build of the fish accentuates the fact that it is a lively swimmer. *Temperature:* 24°C (75°F). *Diet:* prefers live foods, particularly insects, but will take dry foods. *Breeding:* takes place over a period of days; eggs laid in small numbers (2 to 6) at a time.

Harlequin Fish; Red Rasbora *Rasbora heteromorpha* 40 mm 1½ in. Indonesia, Sumatra, Thailand: streams and pools. Perhaps the most popular Rasbora. A red and silver body sporting a blue/black triangular patch. Dorsal and anal fins have red markings. It has been suggested that the sexes may be distinguished by studying the leading outline of the triangular marking, which is said to be more clearly defined in the male. Definitely a fish to be kept in a shoal, where its distinctive coloration may be better appreciated. *Temperature:* 24°C (75°F). *Diet:* all foods. *Breeding:* spawning pattern dissimilar to regular Cyprinids. Eggs are laid on the underside of aquatic plants, where fertilization takes place.

Pigmy Rasbora; Spotted Rasbora
Rasbora maculata 25 mm 1 in. Indonesia, Malaysia: still, and slow-moving waters. The smallest Rasbora. Black patches mark the reddish-brown body, and the fins are red. With its diminutive size, this species may be kept in relatively smaller quarters, and a 30-litre (6-gallon) tank is quite adequate for a community of this species. It should only be kept with fishes of known peaceful temperaments, otherwise its aquarium life may be threatened by larger, more predatory species. *Temperature:* 24°C (75°F). *Diet:* all foods of suitable size. *Breeding:* follows usual pattern, but fry very small.

Red-striped Rasbora; Glowlight Rasbora *Rasbora pauciperforata* 55 mm 2 in. Indonesia: creeks and streams. Another sleek, silvery fish but quite recognizable by the longitudinal iridescent red/gold line from head to caudal fin. The fins may be tinged with yellow. Females may often be larger than the males. Swims in middle and lower water levels. *Temperature:* 24°C (75°F), but will tolerate lower in winter months. *Diet:* sometimes refuses dried foods. *Breeding:* not yet bred in the aquarium.

Scissortail Rasbora; Three-line Rasbora *Rasbora trilineata* 110 mm 4¼ in. Malaysia: still and slow-moving waters. A large fish, a fact not often appreciated by the newcomer when purchasing the smart, silvery fish with the black-marked caudal fin (which twitches so much like the action of scissors). A black line runs from below the dorsal fin horizontally into the caudal fin. Like most Rasboras, this fish is by nature a shoaling fish that swims in the upper levels of the water and takes food from the surface. *Temperature:* 24°C (75°F). *Diet:* all foods, especially insect larvae. *Breeding:* not difficult.

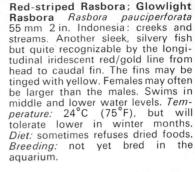

Pygmy Rasbora

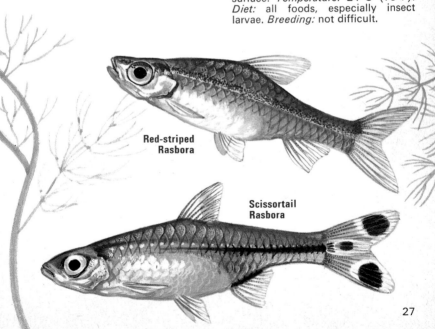

Red-striped Rasbora

Scissortail Rasbora

DANIOS

Danios are hardy and undemanding shoaling fishes similar in habits to the Rasboras. Their sleek lines are often accentuated by horizontal patterning.

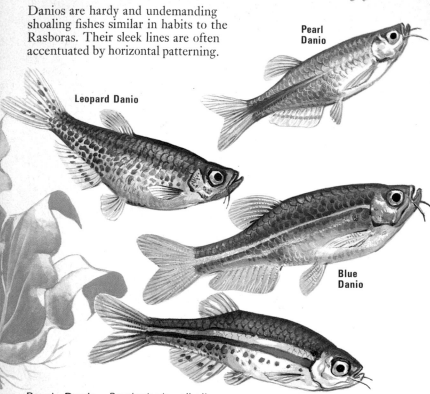

Pearl Danio

Leopard Danio

Blue Danio

Spotted Danio

Pearl Danio *Brachydanio albolineatus* 57 mm 2¼ in. South-east Asia: paddy fields, still and slow-moving waters. An active, medium-sized fish with a blue, pearl lustre to its flanks. A gold horizontal line extends rearwards from below the dorsal fin into the caudal fin and is bordered by blue/violet bands. The fins are yellowish. The beauty of this fish is appreciated better when viewed in reflected light. Females may be recognized by the well-tried method of viewing from above, when their plumpness is easily seen. This fish needs plenty of swimming space. There is a gold variant called the Golden Danio. *Temperature:* 24°C (75°F). *Diet:* all foods. *Breeding:* a ready spawner.

Leopard Danio *Brachydanio frankei* 57 mm 2¼ in. A popular fish, easily recognized by the similarity in markings to its namesake in the mammal kingdom. It may not occur in nature but may have originated in the aquarium as a *sport* (a freak, patterned fish in an otherwise normal spawning of, perhaps, *Brachydanio rerio* or *Brachydanio nigrofasciatus*). Females are noticeably fuller in body depth when ripe. *Temperature:* 24°C (75°F). *Diet:* all foods. *Breeding:* straightforward.

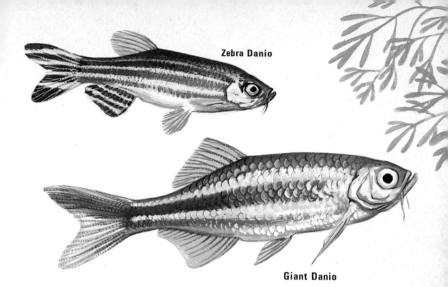

Zebra Danio

Giant Danio

Blue Danio; Kerr's Danio *Brachydanio kerri* 57 mm 2¼ in. Thailand: still and slow-moving waters. A smaller version of the Pearl Danio, but without the same lustre. Blue is the predominant colour and extends into the caudal fin. A gold line runs from the gills to the caudal fin, and there is an accompanying line (often more broken at the anterior end) below it. *Temperature:* 24°C (75°F). *Diet:* all foods. *Breeding:* straightforward.

Spotted Danio; Dwarf Danio *Brachydanio nigrofasciatus* 45 mm 1¾ in. Burma: streams and pools. A dark-blue band runs from behind the gill into the caudal fin, and divides the body coloration into two distinct halves. Above the line a thin gold zone separates the blue line from the brownish back, whilst below, a row of blue-black dots mark the silvery flanks. The anal and ventral fins of the male may be speckled, the female's less so. In recent years, this species has become rare in aquarium circles. *Temperature:* 24°C (75°F). *Diet:* all foods. *Breeding:* straightforward.

Zebra Danio; Zebra Fish *Brachydanio rerio* 50 mm 2 in. Eastern India: paddy fields and slow-moving waters. The most popular and best-known of all the Danios. Its common name describes it precisely: horizontal stripes of royal blue (appearing darker because of their narrowness) cover the silver/gold body from head to tail. The stripes are continued into the fins of the male, but only to a lesser extent in the female. An active fish, and once again a shoal is to be recommended. *Temperature:* 24°C (75°F). *Diet:* all foods. *Breeding:* easy; may be spawned as a shoal.

Giant Danio *Danio malabaricus* 100 mm 4 in. South-west India and Sri Lanka: running waters. A large fish, at first sight almost an enlarged, colour reversal of the Zebra Danio, as it appears to have thin gold stripes on a blue background. The fins may be pinkish-blue. Females may be more rotund than the males. A shoal of these fishes, viewed in reflected light in a large tank, cannot adequately be described by words alone. *Temperature:* 24°C (75°F). *Diet:* all foods, but a varied diet is beneficial. *Breeding:* easy.

29

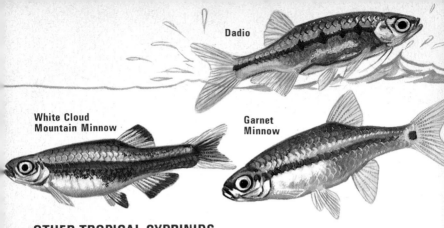

Dadio

White Cloud
Mountain Minnow

Garnet
Minnow

OTHER TROPICAL CYPRINIDS

**White Cloud Mountain Minnow;
Tan's Fish** *Tanichthys albonubes*
45 mm 1¾ in. China: probably running water. A borderline 'tropical', as
it thrives quite happily at lower than
'normal' tropical temperatures. A feature of this fish is its iridescent blue-
green horizontal line, from eye to
caudal fin. The body colour is dark
olive-brown. The fins are yellow,
tipped with red. There is still some
confusion between this fish and
another almost identical species,
Aphyocypris pooni; colour differences
are said to occur in the fins (which
have a red base and yellow margin
tipped with blue in *A. pooni*), but
some sources suggest that the two
fishes are only sub-species of the
same genus. *Temperature:* 16-24°C
(61-75°F). *Diet:* all foods. *Breeding:*
not difficult; may be spawned in
outside ponds in summer as a shoal.
Fry generally ignored by the parents.

Garnet Minnow *Hemigrammo-
cypris lini* 50 mm 2 in. China: probably running waters. A recent addition to the hobby and, at first sight,
may be attributed to the Rasbora
group. A silver-bronze fish with a
dark line running horizontally from
head to caudal fin bordered above
by gold. There is a small dark spot at
the base of the caudal fin. Very active
in the aquarium. *Temperature:* 24°C
(75°F), perhaps slightly lower. *Diet:*
all foods. *Breeding:* although a 'new'
fish, it has proved to be a ready
spawner.

Dadio *Laubuca dadiburjori* 45 mm
1¾ in. Burma, Indonesia, Malaysia,
Sri Lanka, Thailand: paddy fields,
slow-moving waters. A small fish of
golden brown coloration, with a row
of blue spots along the flank joined
by a blue line — very beautiful under
reflected light. The dorsal contour is
flat, with the mouth upturned, indi-
cating a surface feeder. The pectoral
fins are well developed, and may be
used in nature to assist the fish to
'fly' across the water surface and
perhaps even out of the tank. This
species is hardy and colourful, and
looks well in a shoal. *Temperature:*
24°C (75°F), perhaps lower. *Diet:*
live insect food relished, but will
accept dry foods. *Breeding:* spawns
among surface leaves of aquatic
plants, either attaching the eggs
under the leaves or depositing them
in pools of water on top.

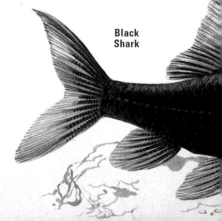

Black
Shark

LARGER TROPICAL CYPRINIDS

Flying Fox *Epalzeorhynchus kallopterus* 140 mm 5½ in. Borneo, Indonesia, Java, Sumatra: densely vegetated creeks. A long, torpedo-shaped fish, with the belly flattened and the mouth underslung. A wide, dark band topped with bright yellow runs horizontally from the snout into the caudal fin. The reddish fins are marked with black areas and tipped with white. Often perches on rocks or broad-leafed plants when at rest. Sometimes takes exception to other members of its own species. *Temperature:* 24°C (75°F). *Diet:* the fringed lips indicate an algae-eating browser, but live and dried foods taken. *Breeding:* not yet bred in the aquarium.

Red-tailed Black Shark *Labeo bicolor* 150 mm 6 in. Thailand: various waters. The large dorsal fin and underslung mouth are responsible for the reference to the shark in the common name, but that this fish is not related to the saltwater species in any way. The rest of the common name, however, describes the fish exactly – everything is black except for the bright, orange-red caudal fin. Can be territorially minded and often attacks intruders. *Temperature:* 25°C (77°F). *Diet:* should include vegetable matter. Often browses on algae and soft-leaved plants. *Breeding:* difficult in the aquarium.

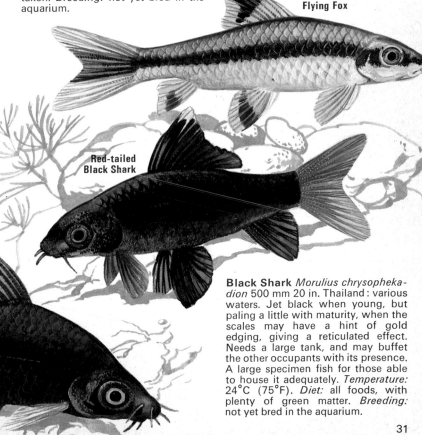

Flying Fox

Red-tailed Black Shark

Black Shark *Morulius chrysophekadion* 500 mm 20 in. Thailand: various waters. Jet black when young, but paling a little with maturity, when the scales may have a hint of gold edging, giving a reticulated effect. Needs a large tank, and may buffet the other occupants with its presence. A large specimen fish for those able to house it adequately. *Temperature:* 24°C (75°F). *Diet:* all foods, with plenty of green matter. *Breeding:* not yet bred in the aquarium.

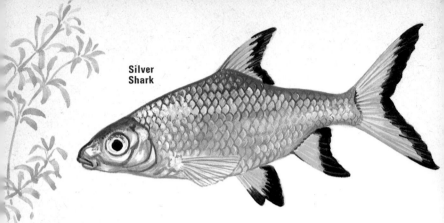

Silver
Shark

Silver Shark; Bala Shark; Tri-color Shark *Balantiocheilus mela-nopterus* 350 mm 13¾ in. Borneo, Sumatra, Thailand: running waters. Although misnamed, a very smart fish. An elongated fish of bluish-silver coloration in general. The main attraction lies in the fins; these are yellow, edged with thick black margins, while the caudal fin also has a red area between the yellow and black. A very fast swimmer, and will also jump. Impressive in shoals. *Temperature:* 24°C (75°F). *Diet:* all foods. *Breeding:* no information available.

Apollo Shark *Luciosoma spilo-pleura* 250 mm 10 in. Indonesia, Malaysia, Thailand, Vietnam: various waters. A Herring-like fish with a regularly interrupted dark line running from snout to caudal fin, where it sweeps upwards to follow the top inside edge. A separate black line follows the edge of the lower lobe of the caudal fin, but is not connected to the main horizontal line. Dark-edged scales above the lateral line give a network effect. All fins have white outside edges. A shoaling fish built for speed. A similar species, *L. setigerum* is also known as the Apollo Shark. Prefers soft, acid water and may be sensitive to water changes. *Temperature:* 24°C (75°F). *Diet:* plenty of insects and other live foods. May prey on smaller fishes. *Breeding:* no information available.

Apollo
Shark

COLDWATER CYPRINIDS

A Stickleback threatens a rival.

Although many native fishes, such as Minnows, Rudd, Sticklebacks and Tench, may be kept in coldwater aquarium conditions with some success, coldwater aquarists usually devote most attention to the culture of various forms of the Goldfish (*Carassius auratus*). Although hardly larger in length than some medium-sized tropical Cyprinids, the Goldfish and its fancy varieties need more oxygen, and the aquarium should be proportionately larger to meet this need.

Bitterling

female spawning

Bitterling *Rhodeus amarus* 80 mm 3¼ in. Europe: various waters. Has a violet, blue-green iridescent sheen to the body. A horizontal blue-green line extends rearwards from below the large dorsal fin to the caudal fin, where it terminates in a red spot. The fins and the eyes may also be reddish. Although it may rival its tropical relations in its colouring, the Bitterling's main attraction to the aquarist is its method of reproduction. Eggs are laid, via a long, extended ovipositor, into the inlet siphon of a freshwater bivalve, the Painter's Mussel or the Swan Mussel. The male Bitterling's fertilizing milt is drawn into the Mussel during its respiratory cycle and fertilization of the eggs occurs. The fry then develop inside the Mussel. The secret of spawning Bitterlings successfully lies in the aquarist's ability to maintain the host Mussel in the aquarium, as the fishes themselves present no problems. *Temperature:* 4-22°C (39-72°F). *Diet:* all foods. *Breeding:* see above.

33

SINGLE-TAILS

Common
Goldfish

Comet

Bristol
Shubunkin

**TWIN-TAILS WITHOUT
DORSAL FIN**

Lionhead

Pompon

Celestial

Bubble-
eye

34

Goldfish *Carassius auratus* Although an aquarium favourite for many years, the common Goldfish is perhaps more suitable for pond life, where it can even survive beneath ice. However, genetic experimentation by aquarists has produced many fascinating Fancy Goldfish varieties that do better in the confines of the aquarium, being too delicate to withstand the rigours of the outdoor pond. Of these varieties, the beginner should gain experience with the singletail species before graduating to the more demanding twintails. Due to their foraging habits when searching for food, the Fancy Goldfish's tank should be furnished with well-rooted plants that are perhaps protected with small pebbles around the crown to prevent uprooting. Undergravel filtration is not suitable for such an aquarium and external or box filters may do a better job of maintaining water clarity. Goldfish are not difficult to feed; in the pond they will eat insects and worms that fall into the pool, whilst in the indoor aquarium live and dried foods, even household scraps, are readily accepted. But, particularly in the case of the more exotic forms, the tank must be kept clean at all times and uneaten food and detritus regularly removed.

TWIN-TAILS WITH DORSAL FIN

Fantail

Veiltail

Oranda

Moor

35

CHARACINS/
FAMILY CHARACIDAE

A large group of fishes containing over 1300 species, some of which are suitable for the aquarium. Most species come from Central and South America, although there are a few representative species from Africa and North America. A family characteristic is the possession of an adipose fin, although some species are without it. All have teeth, more strongly developed in some species than in others. Of carnivorous appetite generally, but a few isolated species may be vegetable or fruit eaters. These brightly coloured fishes are always happier in a shoal and may be induced to spawn in captivity without too much trouble. Although preferring soft, acid water, the fishes are hardy enough to adapt to most domestic water supplies.

Characidae

Neon Tetra

Cardinal Tetra

Cardinal Tetra *Cheirodon axelrodi* 50 mm 2 in. South America: the Amazon and jungle streams. A truly gorgeous fish. An electric-blue-green horizontal stripe runs from snout to adipose fin. Below it a broad band of scarlet covers the rest of the body, with the exception of a silver/white belly. The fins are colourless, except for the caudal, which has some continuation of the red of the body. *Temperature:* 24°C (75°F). *Diet:* all foods. *Breeding:* spawnings have been reported.

Neon Tetra *Paracheirodon innesi* 45 mm 1¾ in. South America: jungle streams. Until the introduction of the Cardinal Tetra, this was the jewel of the aquarium. Colouring is almost identical, except that the red band does not extend the whole length of the body but covers only the rear half. Females may be deeper in the body and, when full of roe, their extra plumpness may cause a visible bend in the blue-green line. *Temperature:* 24°C (75°F). *Diet:* all foods. *Breeding:* has been spawned in as little as a litre (2 pints) of water of various hardnesses.

Silver-tipped Tetra; Copper Tetra
Hasemania marginata 50 mm 2 in.
South America: shallow jungle
streams. A silvery-brown fish of the
standard 'Tetra' shape, with fins
tipped with white. A dark line runs
from below the dorsal fin into the
caudal fin, terminating in a dark
patch. The male fish is a deeper
copper-bronze. Another species,
Hemigrammus nanus, is almost identical, the difference being that *Hasemania* species have no adipose fin.
Temperature: 24°C (75°F). *Diet:* all
foods. *Breeding:* egg scattering. Fry
small and may not be easily visible
for a few days.

Head and Tail Light Tetra;
Beacon Fish *Hemigrammus ocellifer*
45 mm 1¾ in. South America: various
waters. The red/gold eye and the
gold patch at the base of the caudal
fin provide the common name of this
fish. A dark line runs horizontally
along the rear half of the body,
broadening into a dark area at the
base of the caudal fin. The fins may
have blue/white edgings or tips.
Males may have a dark shoulder
patch highlighted by a gold surround.
Temperature: 24°C (75°F). *Diet:*
all foods. *Breeding:* egg scattering.

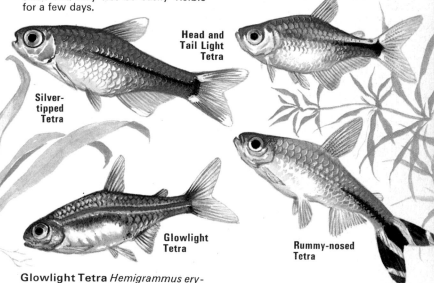

Head and
Tail Light
Tetra

Silver-
tipped
Tetra

Glowlight
Tetra

Rummy-nosed
Tetra

Glowlight Tetra *Hemigrammus ery-*
throzonus (*gracilis*) 45 mm 1¾ in.
Guyana, South America: jungle
streams. Slightly deeper in the body
and more subdued in colouring than
the Neon Tetra. A glowing pink/red
line runs from the snout horizontally
along the body to terminate in a red
area at the base of the caudal fin. The
area above this line is brown, silver
below. The dorsal and anal fins have
a rosy patch and may be tipped with
white. Females are deeper in the
body. *Temperature:* 24°C (75°F).
Diet: all foods. *Breeding:* egg scattering. Soft water for breeding is
advantageous.

Rummy-nosed Tetra; Red-nosed
Tetra *Hemigrammus rhodostomus*
55 mm 2¼ in. South America: jungle
streams. A silvery fish whose main
coloration is provided by the bright
red snout and head and the black and
white, horizontally striped caudal fin.
A thin, dark line runs from below the
dorsal fin into the middle dark stripe
of the caudal fin; another dark line
runs from the anal fin rearwards along
the ventral contour of the body.
Temperature: 24°C (75°F). *Diet:* all
foods. *Breeding:* difficult, because
this is a shy and very sensitive species.

Lemon Tetra *Hyphessobrycon pulchripinnis* 50 mm 2 in. South America: various waters. A delicate lemon-yellow body, with a red iris to the eye. An albino form exists, but only in aquaria. The leading edge of the partially black anal fin is bright yellow. The dorsal fin may have a black edge or tip. *Temperature:* 24°C (75°F). *Diet:* all foods. *Breeding:* possible.

Rosy Tetra; Rosaceous Tetra *Hyphessobrycon rosaceus* 50 mm 2 in. South America: various waters. Pink or rosy body colour, the fins similarly coloured, with the caudal fin having deep red in the lobes. The male's anal fin may be edged with black, and the dorsal is sickle-shaped, black, and tipped with white. Females are deeper in the body. There is some confusion between this species and *H.ornatus. Temperature:* 24°C (75°F). *Diet:* all foods. *Breeding:* possible. A slight rise in temperature may be beneficial.

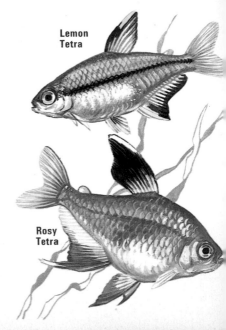

Lemon Tetra

Rosy Tetra

Bleeding Heart Tetra; Tetra Perez
Hyphessobrycon erythrostigma 70 mm 2¾ in. South America: streams and rivers. This larger Tetra has a similar body shape and colouring to the Rosy Tetra, but with the addition of a red spot just behind the gills. There may be a pink/violet band running along the lateral line. The anal fin is white, with a black and pink edging. The dorsal fin (sickle-shaped in the male) is pink/mauve with a black area, and the tip may be white. A dark vertical line crosses the eye.

A striking fish, but it seems to be of a nervous disposition, often being alarmed by the aquarist's presence near the tank. This species was formerly known as *H. rubrostigma.* *Temperature:* 24°C (75°F). *Diet:* all foods. *Breeding:* difficult.

The delicate colours of Bleeding Heart and Rosy Tetras stand out clearly against a dark background. A carefully planned background can enhance the appearance of both fishes and aquarium.

Serpae Tetra *Hyphessobrycon serpae* 45 mm 1¾ in. South America: various waters. A fish which may be classified under several names (*H. callistus, H. bentosi, H. minor*), because the colour patterns vary with age and interbreeding of the species occurs. A blood-red body, with a black-edged anal fin, a black area over most of the dorsal fin, and a black, diamond-shaped mark on the shoulder. In some circles this fish has the reputation of being a fin-nipper of other fishes. *Temperature:* 24°C (75°F). *Diet:* all foods. *Breeding:* possible.

Red Phantom Tetra *Megalamphodus sweglesi* 40 mm 1½ in. South America: various waters. A blushing red colour with red fins and a black, wedge-shaped shoulder patch. Under certain lighting conditions, the fish may appear transparent. *M. melanopterus* is similar in shape and temperament, but is black instead of red. *Temperature:* 24°C (75°F). *Diet:* all foods. *Breeding:* possible.

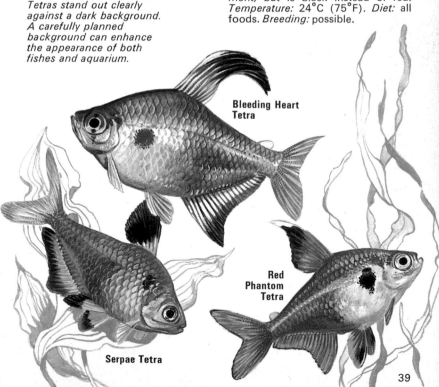

Bleeding Heart
Tetra

Red
Phantom
Tetra

Serpae Tetra

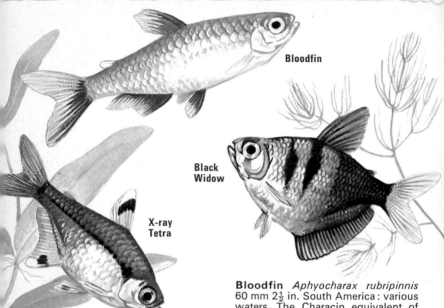

Bloodfin

Black
Widow

X-ray
Tetra

X-ray Tetra; X-ray Fish; Riddle's Tetra *Pristella maxillaris* (*riddlei*) 45 mm 1¾ in. A silvery body colour. The almost transparent body allows internal organs to be seen. The caudal fin is red, the remaining fins yellow and black, tipped with white. A horizontal dark line is sometimes prominent. *Temperature:* 24°C (75°F). *Diet:* all foods. *Breeding:* avid egg eaters, so egg-saving essential.

Black Widow; Petticoat Fish; Blackamoor; Butterfly Tetra *Gymnocorymbus ternetzi* 60 mm 2½ in. South America: various waters. A deep and laterally compressed body, silver in colour with the rear half black. A black vertical stripe passes through the eye. Two black, vertical bars almost cross the body between the gill cover and the dorsal fin. A long-finned variety has recently been introduced. *Temperature:* 24°C (75°F). *Diet:* all foods. *Breeding:* possible.

Bloodfin *Aphyocharax rubripinnis* 60 mm 2½ in. South America: various waters. The Characin equivalent of the Cyprinid shoaling fishes. Active, upper water-level swimmer. Silver body. Ventral and anal fins and lower base of the caudal fin are blood-red. Males have tiny hooks on the anal fin, which occasionally catch in the aquarist's net. An almost identical species, *A. dentatus,* has less red on the caudal fin and is known as the False Bloodfin. *Temperature:* 24°C (75°F). *Diet:* all foods. *Breeding:* egg eaters.

Blind Cave Fish *Astyanax* (formerly *Anoptichthys*) *jordani* 90 mm 3½ in. Mexico: underground waters. Silvery-pink body, and colourless fins. The fry have eyes, but later lose them. The adult fish navigates by sensing vibrations from other fishes, or reflected from obstacles, through its extra-sensitive lateral line system. Fares ably in the community tank despite its lack of vision. Also classified as *A. fasciatus, A. mexicanus* or *A. fasciatus mexicanus. Temperature:* 24°C (75°F), or slightly lower. *Diet:* all foods. *Breeding:* possible. Soft water may be advantageous.

Splashing
Tetra

A Splashing Tetra at rest.

Splashing Tetra; Spraying Characin *Copeina arnoldi* 80 mm 3¼ in. South America : slow-moving waters. The slender, reddish-brown body has a lighter belly region. The dark-edged scales give a reticulated effect to the top half of the body. A dark stripe runs from the snout to behind the gill cover. The fins are yellow with red dots, while the ventral and anal fins may be dark edged. The caudal fin is asymmetric. The dorsal fin has black and white markings. *Temperature:* 24°C (75°F). *Diet:* insects and dried foods. *Breeding:* lays eggs above the water surface on the underside of overhanging plant leaf. A cover glass may be used as a substitute in the aquarium. The male splashes the eggs to prevent dehydration. Other species of *Copeina* (also referred to as *Copella*) spawn on submerged plant leaves or in pits scooped in the aquarium gravel.

Blind Cave
Fish

Emperor Tetra *Nematobrycon palmeri* 60 mm 2½ in. South America: streams and rivers. A relatively new fish introduced in the 1960s. A silver-grey body with a dark back. A black band surmounted by blue/turquoise runs from the head to the caudal fin, where the black band continues through to the extended central rays. The male's dorsal fin is sickle-shaped with extended first rays coloured black; the male also has more and longer extensions to the caudal fin than the female. The anal fin has a black margin edged with yellow. The eyes of the male are blue, those of the female green. Males threaten each other, but no violence is done. *Temperature:* 24°C (75°F). *Diet:* all foods. *Breeding:* possible, producing 50 to 100 fry.

Congo Tetra; Congo Salmon *Phenacogrammus interruptus* 90 mm 3½ in. Africa: Zaire River area. Ideal for a one-species tank; does well in a shoal. The body colour is a metallic blue-green with a broad, gold, iridescent band running from the eye to the adipose fin. Large, dark-edged scales. Females are drabber. The male has elongated central rays of the caudal fin, and the dorsal fin often trails over the caudal peduncle. When seen against a dark background the fins appear to be outlined with white. *Temperature:* 24°C (75°F). *Diet:* insects, dried food and duckweed. *Breeding:* eggs laid over a period of days. Eggs may be delicate, because of their sensitivity to the water chemistry.

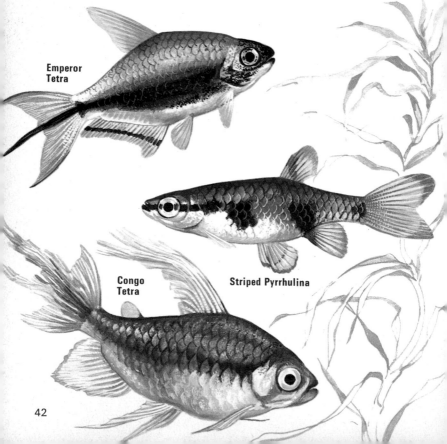

Emperor Tetra

Congo Tetra

Striped Pyrrhulina

Striped Pyrrhulina *Pyrrhulina vittata* 70 mm 2¾ in. South America: slow-moving waters. Elongated, golden-brown body, with a horizontal dark line running from the snout to just behind the gill cover. Three dark, uneven, vertical marks cross the body between the mid-position and the caudal fin. The dorsal fin has a dark blotch. The caudal fin is asymmetric. *Temperature:* 24°C (75°F). *Diet:* insects, but all foods taken. *Breeding:* eggs deposited on leaves. The male guards the eggs.

Penguin Fish *Thayeria obliqua* 65 mm 2½ in. South America: running waters. A plain, silver-brown body. The main feature is a black line on the rear part of the body which follows into the lower lobe of the caudal fin. The fins may be white-tipped. Has a habit of resting at an angle of 45° with a 'tail-down' attitude. Other species of *Thayeria* are distinguished only by differences in the black markings. *Temperature:* 24°C (75°F). *Diet:* all foods. *Breeding:* very prolific, but eggs may be attacked by micro-organisms in the water, because natural waters have a high humus — and hence a low bacterial — content.

The Congo Tetra, one of the few Characins from Africa, has large reflective scales, and the male fish has well-developed, white-edged fins.

Penguin Fish

LARGER CHARACINS

Bucktoothed Tetra; Exodon *Exodon paradoxus* 139 mm 5 in. South America : various waters. An attractive and active fish, but is very aggressive and should only be kept in a large, thickly planted tank with fishes that are able to look after themselves. Has a gold metallic body, with two large black blotches. The fins are yellow with patches of red. *Temperature:* 24°C (75°F). *Diet:* all foods, including greenstuffs. *Breeding:* no details available.

Schreitmuller's Metynnis *Metynnis schreitmulleri* 140 mm 5½ in. South America : slow-moving waters. Has a silvery, disc-shaped body, a broad-based adipose fin, and a serrated keel. During the breeding period, the female has a red edge to the anal fin, while the male's is black. A very striking fish in a shoal, but needs a large tank. Often suspected of having the same carnivorous tendencies as the Piranha but, along with *Colossoma* and *Mylossoma* species, is a vegetable and fruit eater. *Temperature:* 24°C (75°F). *Diet:* usually vegetable matter and fruit, but will take live foods. *Breeding:* possible, but the number of young may reach into thousands.

Glass Tetra; Red-eyed Tetra *Moenkhausia oligolepis* 120 mm 4¾ in. South America : various waters. An attractive fish when young, but often grows larger than anticipated. Silver-grey, with dark-edged scales. The eye is bright red in the top half, gold below. A yellow-gold band crosses the caudal peduncle and is accentuated by the white-edged black base of the caudal fin. The other fins may be white-tipped. Females are deeper in the body. A similar species, *M. sanctae filomenae* does not grow so large (70 mm 2¾ in.). *Temperature:* 24°C (75°F). *Diet:* all foods. *Breeding:* prolific.

Red Piranha; Natterer's Piranha *Rooseveltiella nattereri* 300 mm 11¾ in. South America : various waters. One look at the teeth of this species is enough to convince the aquarist of the truth of stories about these carnivorous fishes. A disc-shaped, muscular fish with steel-grey colouring flecked with sparkling scales. The belly and throat regions are orange/red. The dorsal and caudal fins are grey, the caudal fin having a dark edge; the anal fin is red with a dark edge. Obviously, a candidate for the large aquarium when adult, but young specimens can be kept together from a young age until the first signs of trouble. *Temperature:* 24°C (75°F). *Diet:* young fishes, lean meat or meat-based flake foods, or insects. *Breeding:* occasional spawnings have been reported, but details unknown.

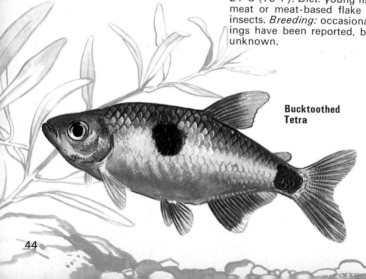

Bucktoothed Tetra

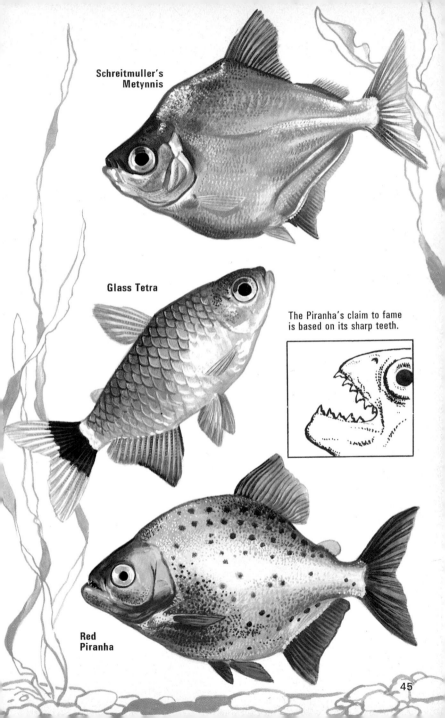

Schreitmuller's
Metynnis

Glass Tetra

The Piranha's claim to fame
is based on its sharp teeth.

Red
Piranha

45

Anostomidae

RELATED SPECIES

The following species may be considered to be closely related to the Characidae and are usually included in the same competitive class by hobbyists.

HEADSTANDERS/ FAMILY ANOSTOMIDAE

The characteristic 'head-down' attitude adopted by these fishes when resting is probably an extension of the swimming position when searching for food, or a protective camouflage among plants.

Marbled Head-stander

Striped Headstander

Marbled Headstander *Abramites microcephalus* 130 mm 5 in. South America: slow-moving waters. A larger, stockier fish than its relatives. Seven or eight broad dark bands cross the body vertically, the central band continuing across the dorsal and ventral fins. The other fins are yellow-brown. The head is very small, and a dark band crosses the eye obliquely. A shy fish, but has a reputation of being a fin-nipper and eater of soft-leaved plants. *Temperature:* 24°C (75°F). *Diet:* worms preferred, and greenstuffs. *Breeding:* no details available.

Striped Headstander; Striped Anostomus *Anostomus anostomus* 140 mm 5½ in. South America: slow-moving waters. Has a cigar-shaped body. Three broad, parallel, dark bands run horizontally down the length of the body; spaces between the bands are yellow-gold. The fins are red and the mouth small. Rests in a vertical position. *Temperature:* 24°C (75°F). *Diet:* all foods including vegetable matter. *Breeding:* no details available.

Spotted Headstander *Chilodus punctatus* 75 mm 3 in. South America: slow-moving waters. Not quite so deep-bodied as the Marbled Headstander. The scales have dark spots giving a checkered appearance. A dark line runs from the snout and

Night Tetra

Banded Leporinus

Spotted Headstander

continues through the eye to the gill cover through to the caudal fin. The large, square-shaped dorsal fin has a black blotch. The eye is red. Swims head down. Shy, but may quarrel with its own species. *Temperature:* 24°C (75°F). *Diet:* all foods, including greenstuffs. *Breeding:* no details available.

Banded Leporinus; Striped Leporinus *Leporinus fasciatus* 300 mm 11¾ in. South America: slow-moving waters. Has a long, cylindrical body, yellow in colour and ringed with several dark bands beginning through the eye and ending at the caudal fin. The name Leporinus refers to the shape of the mouth, which is hare-like (*Leporinus* is Latin for a young hare). These fishes are good jumpers, so a glass cover is obligatory. *Temperature:* 24°C (75°F). *Diet:* must contain greenstuffs, otherwise soft-leaved plants will suffer. *Breeding:* no information available.

Night Tetra; Flagtailed Prochilodus *Prochilodus insignis* 250 mm 10 in. South America: various waters. Has a silver body with a bluish-green sheen. The caudal and anal fins have horizontal dark blue and white stripes. The dorsal fin may have blue stripes. The other fins are reddish. This fish is an excellent jumper and prefers to be in a shoal. *Temperature:* 24°C (75°F). *Diet:* green foods and some live foods. *Breeding:* not yet bred in the aquarium.

47

Distichodus

FAMILY CITHARINIDAE

A small group of African fishes closely related to the Characidae. *Distochodus* and *Nannaethiops* are the most commonly kept species; others are too large or aggressive.

One-striped African Characin

Citharinidae

Marbled Hatchetfish

Distichodus *Distichodus lusosso* 330 mm 13 in. Central Africa : various waters. A magnificent specimen fish for the large aquarium. Red-gold colouring with the dark-edged scales individually picked out. Six or seven transverse dark stripes cross the body at equal intervals. The fins are bright red, with the caudal fin edged with black. Has a long snout. *Temperature:* 24°C (75°F). *Diet:* live foods preferred, but will accept dried foods and vegetable matter, including soft-leaved plants. *Breeding:* not yet bred in the aquarium.

One-striped African Characin *Nannaethiops unitaeniatus* 65 mm 2½ in. Central Africa : various waters. A silvery-yellow fish with a dark horizontal line, surmounted with gold, running from the snout to the caudal fin. Females are deeper in the body. Males may have red fins, particularly dorsal and anal fins, during the breeding period. Peaceful, often shy. *Temperature:* 24°C (75°F). *Diet:* all foods. Comes out of hiding for worms. *Breeding:* prolific.

Common Hatchetfish

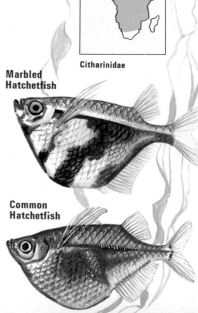

Half-lined Hemiodus

HATCHETFISHES/ FAMILY GASTEROPELECIDAE

These are hatchet-shaped, deep-bodied fishes, strongly compressed laterally. They can fly short distances across the water surface, using fins resembling those of the Flying Fish.

Gasteropelecidae   Hemiodontidae

Marbled Hatchetfish *Carnegiella strigata* 65 mm 2½ in. South America: slow-moving waters. The fish's deep body shape is necessary to accommodate the enlarged muscles that control the movement of the well-developed pectoral fins. A silver fish with attractive marbled patterning below a single, gold horizontal stripe. A glass cover on the tank is essential. *Temperature:* 26°C (79°F). *Diet:* insects and floating foods. *Breeding:* possible, but no information published.

Common Hatchetfish *Gasteropelecus sternicla* 65 mm 2½ in. South America: slow-moving waters. A plain, silver fish, with all the physical features of the Marbled Hatchetfish except the marbled patterning. A dark horizontal line extends from behind the gill cover to the caudal fin. The Silver Hatchetfish (*G. levis*) is almost identical, but may have a dark blotch at the base of the dorsal fin. A surface dweller. *Temperature:* 26°C (79°F). *Diet:* insects, floating foods. *Breeding:* not yet bred in the aquarium.

FAMILY HEMIODONTIDAE

These are South American fishes distinguished from the Characidae by the lack of teeth in the lower jaw. In America, this group is known as Lebiasinidae.

Half-lined Hemiodus; Silver Hemiodus; Flying Swallow *Hemiodopsis* (formerly *Hemiodus*) *semitaeniatus* 200 mm 7¾ in. South America: various waters. A very streamlined, silver fish. A dark spot is situated on the flank between the dorsal and adipose fins. After a gap, a dark line runs into the caudal fin, following a downward direction midway through the lower lobe. A fast swimmer, and loves a shoaling existence. Very attractive when young but grows rapidly. *Temperature:* 24°C (75°F), or slightly lower. *Diet:* all foods. *Breeding:* not yet bred in the aquarium.

PENCILFISHES

During recent years, the *Nannostomus* genus has been the subject of some re-classification with, first, the *Poeciliobrycon* division being created and, now, the *Nannobrycon* genus being suggested for all fishes in this group. All Pencilfishes have small mouths, but not all have adipose fins; again, some, but not all, swim at an oblique angle. Males constantly 'threaten' each other with a fine display of fin stretching, and they similarly perform in front of the females. The Pencilfishes have a family characteristic of nocturnal coloration, and the aquarist may be surprised to see them looking different early in the morning; descriptions in the text refer to normal daylight colours.

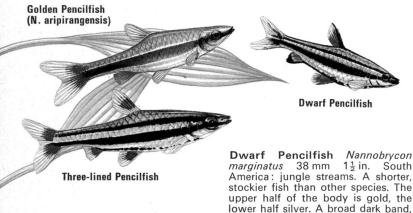

**Golden Pencilfish
(N. aripirangensis)**

Dwarf Pencilfish

Three-lined Pencilfish

Golden Pencilfish; One-lined Pencilfish *Nannobrycon beckfordi* 50 mm 2 in. South America: jungle streams. Several attempts have been made to sub-divide this species further on a colour-pattern basis. The golden-bodied form with a single, dark horizontal line, red anal fin and red lower caudal fin has been known as *H. beckfordi anomalus*. The form with a red band alongside the dark band, and red at the base of the caudal fin, may be known as *N. beckfordi aripirangensis*. There is also *N. beckfordi beckfordi*, the Golden Pencilfish, measuring 65 mm (2½ in.) long. Males often spar with each other. *Temperature:* 26°C (79°F). *Diet:* all suitably proportioned foods. *Breeding:* adults are egg eaters. Sometimes water conditions do not favour development of the eggs.

Dwarf Pencilfish *Nannobrycon marginatus* 38 mm 1½ in. South America: jungle streams. A shorter, stockier fish than other species. The upper half of the body is gold, the lower half silver. A broad dark band, edged above with red, runs from the snout to the caudal fin. Another two black lines parallel this band on either side. The dorsal and anal fins are red, edged in black; the ventral fins are white with a red patch. *Temperature:* 26°C (79°F). *Diet:* all foods. *Breeding:* adults are egg eaters.

Three-lined Pencilfish *Nannobrycon trifasciatus* 50 mm 2 in. South America: jungle streams. A 'stretched' version of the Dwarf Pencilfish. Other differences occur in the colour pattern of the fins: the base of the caudal fin has two red patches separated by an over-run of the body colour. The dorsal, anal and ventral fins are clear with red patches. *Temperature:* 26°C (79°F). *Diet:* all foods. *Breeding:* possible, but more difficult than other Pencilfishes, because natural waters are very high in humus content.

LOACHES/
FAMILY COBITIDAE

Members of this family are bottom–dwelling fishes, and may be recognized as such by their flat ventral profile and underslung mouths, complete with barbels. In the aquarium, Loaches may be nocturnal, although some soon lose their shyness and venture around the tank during its illuminated periods. The fishes often make hiding places themselves by burrowing under rocks or into a tangle of aquarium plants. Most prefer to live in a community rather than as solitary specimens. The majority of Loaches have erectile spines, a defence weapon mainly, and these may catch in the aquarist's net. There are many varieties to choose from, each with a differing colour pattern or body form, but they are all difficult to catch with a net.

Kuhli Loach; Coolie Loach *Acanthophthalmus kuhli* 110 mm 4½ in. South-east Asia: streams and rivers. This genus gets its name, meaning 'thorn-eye', from the spine over the eye. It has a worm-like body, flattened laterally at the caudal peduncle, and an underslung mouth with barbels. A pink/yellow coloration, with two or three dark bands encircling the head and gill cover. A large number of dark bands (often split longitudinally) almost ring the rest of the body, but do not cover the belly. The fins are colourless. Frequents tangles of plant roots and may form a tangled mass with its brothers and sisters. Several species of *Acanthophthalmus* are available. *Temperature:* 24°C (75°F). *Diet:* worms, but will scavenge for other foods. *Breeding:* possible.

Nichols' Loach *Noemacheilus nicholsi* 65 mm 2½ in. India, Far East: slow-moving waters. Has a cylindrical body shape, but its finnage is more conventional than in *Acanthophthalmus*. A number of vertical dark bands ring the red/brown body almost completely. A narrow, dark band crosses the caudal peduncle and there is a small, dark dot at the base of the dorsal fin. Fond of perching on its ventral and anal fins when at rest. *Temperature:* 24°C (75°F). *Diet:* worms preferred, but usual foods taken. *Breeding:* not yet bred in the aquarium.

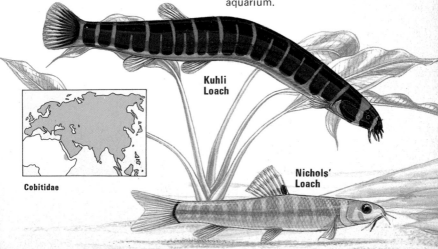

Kuhli
Loach

Cobitidae

Nichols'
Loach

Skunk Botia; Hora's Loach; Mouse Loach *Botia horae* 90 mm 3½ in. Indonesia : slow-moving waters. An attractive smaller Loach in this group. A grey/green body with a dark line running from the snout along the top of the back and crossing the body immediately in front of the caudal fin. The scales are very small, and fishes of this genus appear to have a matt finish. Some may have thin transverse lines on the flanks. The erectile spine is carried below the eye. A fairly active fish, but it may be timid if alone in a community collection. *Temperature:* 24°C (75°F). *Diet:* prefers worms and insect larvae, but will take dried foods, often in mid-water. *Breeding:* no information available.

Pakistani Loach; Reticulated Loach *Botia lohachata* 110 mm 4½ in. India and Pakistan : slow-moving waters. A very striking Loach. The body colour is silver/grey with Y-shaped dark markings on the flanks, interspersed with black blotches. The patterning is continued into the fins. An active fish, more so at evening times, which burrows under rocks and plants. *Temperature:* 24°C (75°F). *Diet:* as for *B. horae. Breeding:* not yet bred in the aquarium.

Clown Loach; Tiger Botia *Botia macracantha* 200 mm 8 in. Indonesia : slow-moving waters. A very attractive fish. Three black bands encircle the bright orange body. The dorsal and anal fins are black with orange edges ; the other fins are red, with streaks of black in the caudal fin. Susceptible to White Spot disease, and some sources suggest that medicants are not well tolerated. This species grows much larger in nature. *Temperature:* 24°C (75°F). *Diet:* as for *B. horae. Breeding:* not yet bred in the aquarium regularly, but spawning has been reported.

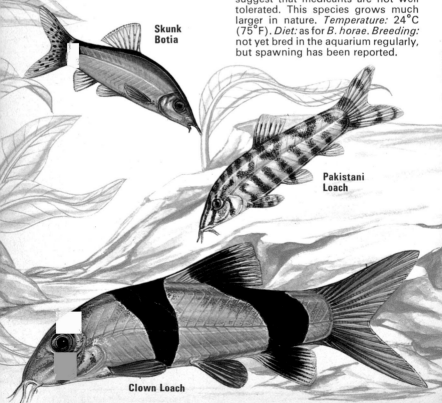

Skunk Botia

Pakistani Loach

Clown Loach

Orange-finned Loach *Botia modesta* 190 mm 7½ in. Malay peninsula, Thailand : slow-moving waters. Has a steel-blue/grey body with a vague dark blotch immediately in front of the caudal fin. The fins may be yellow or orange. Often confused with *B. lecontei*, but most sources agree that *B. modesta* is the stockier fish. *Temperature:* 24°C (75°F). *Diet:* as for *B. horae. Breeding:* not yet bred in the aquarium.

Chain Loach; Dwarf Loach *Botia sidthimunki* 55 mm 2¼ in. Far East : slow-moving waters. The smallest of the Botias, this species has a gold body marked with a dark, chain-link pattern down to midway across the flanks. The lower links may join to form a horizontal line. The fins are clear, except for the caudal fin, which bears some patterning. Less timid than other Loaches, it enjoys the company of its own species. *Temperature:* 24°C (75°F). *Diet:* all foods. *Breeding:* not yet bred in the aquarium.

Zebra Loach *Botia striata* 85 mm 3½ in. India : slow-moving waters. The body is covered in a large number of narrow, dark stripes. The snout is not so pointed as in other species. The fins are patterned. A slow-growing species. Fairly shy, often given up for dead due to its non-appearance, but a hardy fish. *Temperature:* 24°C (75°F). *Diet:* as for *B. horae. Breeding:* not yet bred in the aquarium.

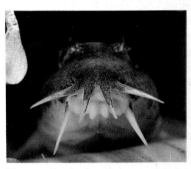

The mouth of a Loach.

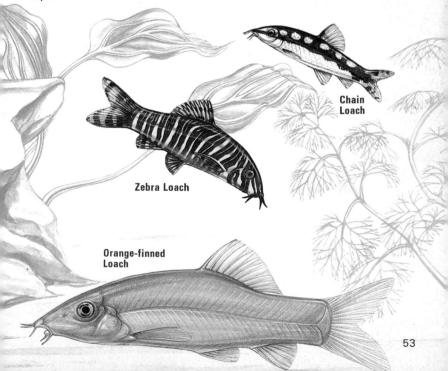

Chain Loach

Zebra Loach

Orange-finned Loach

A Sucking Loach eating algae.

Gyrinocheilidae

Sucking
Loach
on aquarium
glass

FAMILY GYRINOCHEILIDAE

Despite its common names, this fish is neither a Loach nor from China. It is included in this section for easy reference. It is possibly more closely related to the Cyprinidae.

Sucking Loach; Chinese Algae Eater *Gyrinocheilus aymonieri* 250 mm 10 in. Thailand: various waters. This fish is similar to the coldwater Gudgeon (*Gobio gobio*), with a grey-brown body covered in connecting blotches. Some scales have dark centres giving a dotted effect. The fish also has large, fleshy, under-slung lips. It can cling to the glass walls of the aquarium to rasp off algae, and breathes through a special opening in the head whilst doing so. It can become annoyingly territorially-minded, and often quite aggressive towards other fishes. Its efficiency as an algae-remover tends to diminish with maturity. *Temperature:* 24°C (75°F). *Diet:* plenty of vegetable matter, but will eat other foods. *Breeding:* not yet bred in the aquarium.

CATFISHES/SUB-ORDER SILUROIDEA

The sub-Order Siluroidea contains the Catfishes of the aquarium world. With their extended barbels around the mouth, the origin of their common group name can be understood. The smaller 'armoured' Catfishes from South America are covered with overlapping large plates instead of the more usual scales, but the Catfishes from Africa have neither, their skin being quite unprotected.

With their flattened bellies, barbels (which may incorporate taste buds) and often large eyes, it is no surprise that these fishes frequent riverbeds searching for food in semi-darkness. Many are nocturnal by nature. In length, they range from 50 mm (2 in) to 600 mm (24 in) or more. Social habits range from peaceful to predatory, and diets from vegetarian to carnivorous. Catfishes are often kept purely as scavengers and subsequently neglected. They should be considered more favourably, as the species within this group offer the aquarist a wide range of interests; some hobbyists may specialize in these fishes to the exclusion of other families. There are national societies devoted to the study of Catfishes in Britain and the United States.

ARMOURED CATFISHES/ FAMILY CALLICHTHYIDAE

Callichthyidae

Armoured Catfish; Hassar; Bubblenest Catfish *Callichthys callichthys* 180 mm 7¼ in. South America: various waters. The body of this species has hardly any taper. Its head is fairly pointed, the barbels well developed. Two rows of overlapping plates cover the body. The caudal fin is rounded, and the first rays of the adipose, dorsal and pectoral fins are thickened into spines and may have a reddish tinge. Because this is a continually rummaging fish, the aquarium should have a filter system capable of dealing with the resulting suspended matter in the water. *Temperature:* 24°C (75°F). *Diet:* all foods. *Breeding:* bubblenest builder among surface leaves of plants.

Armoured Catfish

55

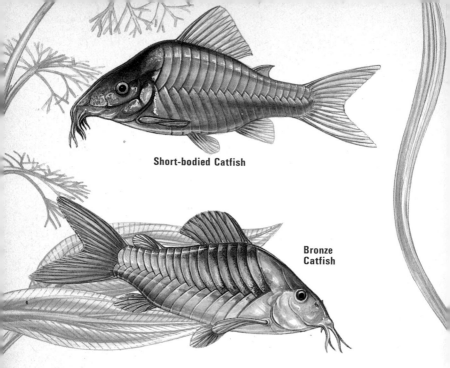

Short-bodied Catfish

Bronze
Catfish

Short-bodied Catfish *Brochis splendens* (*coeruleus*) 76 mm 3 in. South America: slow-moving waters. Has a flat ventral profile and an arched back. The dorsal fin is long-based. The fins are brownish, and the body colour bronze/green. Very similar to the *Corydoras* genus but generally larger; the length of the dorsal fin is conclusive evidence. *Temperature:* 24°C (75°F). *Diet:* all foods; worms relished. *Breeding:* has been bred; probably follows *Corydoras* pattern.

Bronze Catfish *Corydoras aeneus* 75 mm 3 in. South America: various waters. A very popular Catfish, from an equally popular genus. A yellow/reddish/brown body with a dark blue-green metallic sheen on the head and running horizontally along the flanks. The fins are plain and red-brown. Females may be distinguished by the wider cross-section behind the pectoral fins when seen from above. This species often makes a sudden dash to the water surface to gulp air, which is then absorbed in the gut. It is always foraging for food around the aquarium floor and, as a result, the barbels may be worn away through constant digging. Smooth gravel should be used if a community of *Corydoras* is to be kept. Also, by keeping the fishes well fed, the need for them to dig for food will be obviated. *Temperature:* 24°C (75°F). *Diet:* all foods, but worms relished. *Breeding:* lays eggs on plant leaves or tank glass. Female carries fertilized eggs between ventral fins to selected spawning site. Addition of cooler water to the aquarium may induce spawning.

The other species of *Corydoras* (illustrated opposite) include the Elegant Catfish (*C. elegans*, 57 mm), the Dwarf, or Pygmy, Corydoras (*C. hastatus*, 25 mm), the Leopard Corydoras (*C. julii*, 65 mm), the Black-spotted Corydoras (*C. melanistius*, 65 mm), the Peppered Corydoras (*C. paleatus*, 75 mm) and Schwartz's Corydoras (*C. schwartzi*, 65 mm).

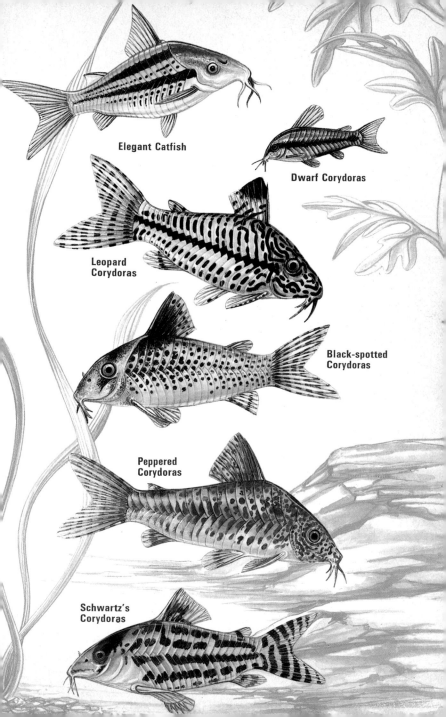

Elegant Catfish

Dwarf Corydoras

Leopard Corydoras

Black-spotted Corydoras

Peppered Corydoras

Schwartz's Corydoras

Port Hoplo; Atipa *Hoplosternum thoracutum* 190 mm 7¼ in. South America: various waters. Has a thickset, almost cylindrical body, grey-brown in colour, with numerous dark blotches. The fins are similarly marked, the caudal fin being pale at the base and rounded. The barbels are long. A similar species is *H. littorale,* but this has a forked caudal fin. *Temperature:* 24°C (75°F). *Diet:* all foods. *Breeding:* bubblenest builder.

Stripe-tailed Catfish *Dianema urostriata* 130 mm 5¼ in. Brazil: various waters. The streamlined body is grey-brown with some dark speckling. A dark line runs from the snout to the rear edge of the gill cover. The barbels are dark, and the adipose fin has a dark edge. The large, black and white caudal fin is horizontally striped. This fish is a midwater swimmer. A similar species, *D. longibarbis,* lacks the spectacular caudal fin markings. *Temperature:* 24°C (75°F). *Diet:* all foods. *Breeding:* no details available.

SUCKER CATFISHES/ FAMILY LORICARIIDAE

The typical underslung mouths of these fishes are used as a means of locomotion and anchorage, as well as for feeding, in fast-flowing waters.

Sucker Catfish; Plecostomus *Hypostomus* (formerly *Plecostomus*) *plecostomus* 450 mm 18 in. South America: various waters. The long, wedge-shaped body is covered with bony plates, which may be in three or four ridged layers, instead of only two as in *Corydoras.* The body is dark brown with darker speckles. The dorsal fin is large and sail-like, while the caudal fin is asymmetric, with the lower lobe larger. A shy and retiring fish, but often dashes out for food. An ideal algae-remover that does not damage plants. *Temperature:* 24°C (75°F). *Diet:* all foods, but greenstuffs should predominate. *Breeding:* no details available.

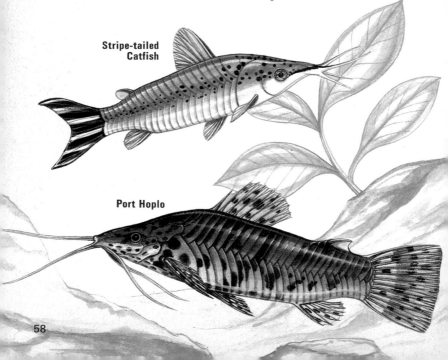

Stripe-tailed Catfish

Port Hoplo

Midget Sucker Catfish *Otocinclus affinis* 50 mm 2 in. South America: various waters. This miniature version of the sucking type of Catfish, has a broad, flattened head and tapering body. A dark line runs from the snout into the caudal fin, terminating as a black patch. The dorsal and anal fins are patterned. The back has dark blotches, while the belly is pale. This fish is often seen clinging to aquarium glass. It prefers a shoal of its own kind. *Temperature:* 24°C (75°F). *Diet:* mainly vegetable matter and worms, but will scavenge for scraps. *Breeding:* has been bred in the aquarium, and follows *Corydoras* pattern.

Whiptail Catfish *Rhinoloricaria* (formerly *Loricaria*) *parva* 130 mm 5¼ in. South America: various waters. The elongated body tapers into almost matchstick proportions. Filaments from the outside rays of the caudal fin are very extended. The body colour is grey-green with some transverse dark markings. The fins are patterned. A bottom-living fish, which often clings to rocks. It can control the amount of light entering the eye by covering the pupil as required. *Temperature:* 24°C (75°F). *Diet:* mainly vegetable matter, but other foods taken. *Breeding:* eggs are laid by the female on a pre-selected site; the male guards the eggs and young.

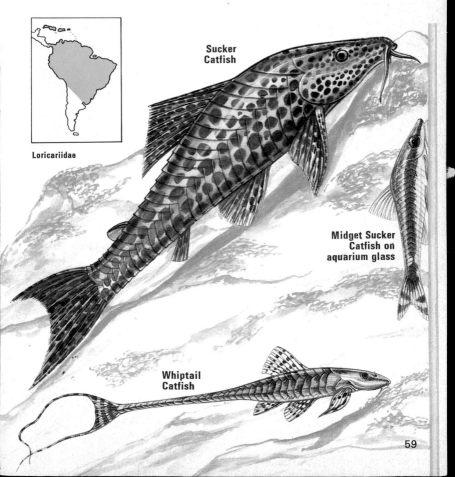

Loricariidae

Sucker Catfish

Midget Sucker Catfish on aquarium glass

Whiptail Catfish

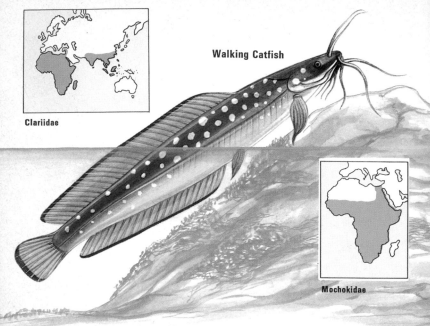

Walking Catfish

Clariidae

Mochokidae

FAMILY CLARIIDAE

Members of this family often leave the water in search of food and can survive long periods out of water. They are often kept for their novelty value.

Walking Catfish; Albino Clarias *Clarias batrachus* 610 mm 28½ in. Far East : various waters. The torpedo-shaped, snake-like body is brown-green with pale dots, and has very long dorsal and anal fins. The dorsal fin may be patterned with dark dots. A pink 'albino' form exists and is a favourite with aquarists. The species can live for long periods out of water, and can travel overland 'walking' on its ventral fins. The tank should be kept securely covered. This fish can also be dangerous to small fishes. *Temperature:* 24°C (75°F). *Diet:* eats anything and becomes very distended. *Breeding:* not yet bred in the aquarium.

AFRICAN CATFISHES/ FAMILY MOCHOKIDAE

The *Synodontis* group have long barbels and long-based adipose fins. The dorsal fins are often large but not always displayed to best advantage. The caudal fins are deeply forked. A generic characteristic is the possession of lockable spines in the pectoral and dorsal fins, which may be erected when the fish is netted or driven into a hiding place.

Polka Dot African Catfish *Synodontis angelicus* 190 mm 7½ in. Africa : slow-moving waters. The young *S. angelicus* is very colourful, being violet with white dots. The adult form is grey with dark blotches. The fins are striped. *Temperature:* 24°C (75°F). *Diet:* live foods, especially worms, and vegetable matter. *Breeding:* not yet bred in the aquarium.

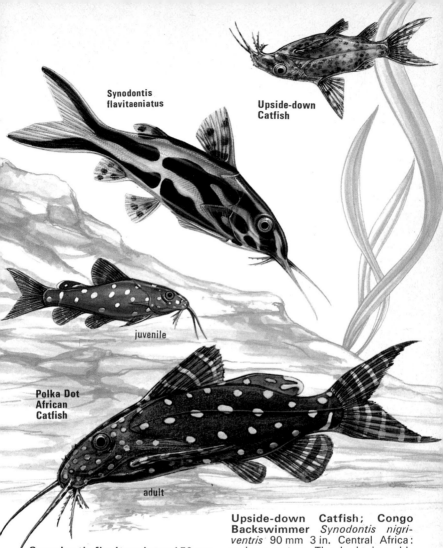

Synodontis flavitaeniatus

Upside-down Catfish

juvenile

Polka Dot African Catfish

adult

Synodontis flavitaeniatus 150 mm 6 in. Africa: various waters. A very striking fish, with a series of light-coloured wavy lines running along the dark body. The fins are patterned with dots. The dorsal fin has a cream leading edge; the caudal fin has cream, dark-bordered edges. *Temperature:* 24°C (75°F). *Diet:* as for *S. angelicus. Breeding:* has been bred in the aquarium, but details unknown.

Upside-down Catfish; Congo Backswimmer *Synodontis nigriventris* 90 mm 3 in. Central Africa: various waters. The body is gold-brown with numerous dark spots; the fins are similarly marked. This species has a habit of swimming upside-down. To assist in its camouflage, the dark patterning is continued on the underside of the fish. *Temperature:* 24°C (75°F). *Diet:* should include greenstuffs. Will take food from water surface while upside-down. *Breeding:* has been bred in the aquarium, but details unknown.

61

FAMILY PIMELODIDAE

This family of unarmoured Catfishes is almost the South American equivalent to the African Mochokidae in appearance.

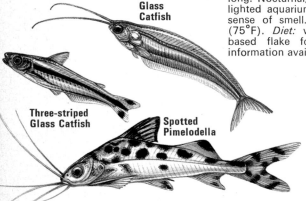

Glass Catfish

Three-striped Glass Catfish

Spotted Pimelodella

Spotted Pimelodella *Pimelodus* (formerly *Pimelodella*) *pictus* 110 mm 4½ in. South America : various waters. An elongated fish of silvery-white colour with numerous black, oval dots on the flanks and caudal fin. The adipose fin is large, with a black tip. The other fins are black-marked to some degree. The barbels are very long. Nocturnal, but will adjust to a lighted aquarium, and has an acute sense of smell. *Temperature:* 24°C (75°F). *Diet:* worms, meat, meat-based flake foods. *Breeding:* no information available.

Pimelodidae

GLASS CATFISHES/ FAMILY SCHILBEIDAE

Although from different families, the two genera of Catfishes described here resemble each other with their transparent bodies.

Schilbeidae

Siluridae

FAMILY SILURIDAE

Three-striped Glass Catfish *Eutropiella debauwi* 70 mm 2¾ in. Central Africa : various waters. The body colour is blue-grey. Three dark, horizontal stripes run from behind the gill cover along the body ; the central line runs through the caudal fin, and continuations of the upper and lower lines appear in the lobes. The anal fin is very long. The dorsal fin is small and carried near the front of the fish. An adipose fin is present. A very active shoaling fish that swims at an oblique angle. *Temperature:* 24°C (75°F). *Diet:* live foods preferred. *Breeding:* not yet bred in the aquarium.

Glass Catfish *Kryptopterus bicirrhis* 90 mm 3½ in. Indonesia, Thailand : shallow waters. Has a totally transparent body with the internal organs enclosed in a silvery sac. The anal fin is very long, while the dorsal fin is reduced to a single ray. The caudal fin is forked and often asymmetric. Swims at an oblique angle, with the tail down. A not too active fish that prefers a peaceful tank and the company of a shoal. A similar species is the slightly larger Poor Man's Glass Catfish (*K. macrocephalus*). *Temperature:* 24°C (75°C). *Diet:* live foods preferred. *Breeding:* not yet bred in the aquarium.

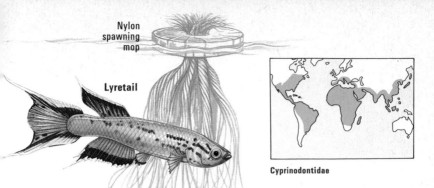

Nylon spawning mop

Lyretail

Cyprinodontidae

EGGLAYING TOOTHCARPS; KILLIFISHES/ FAMILY CYPRINODONTIDAE

The Egglaying Toothcarps comprise mainly the so-called 'annual' fishes whose natural watery habitat completely dries up every year, thus killing the fishes. However, before this event occurs, the adult fishes lay their fertilized eggs in the mud of the stream bed, where they survive the rest of the dry season in a dormant state. The onset of the rainy season refills the stream bed and the eggs hatch. The fish then have to mature and spawn in their turn before the weather cycle is repeated. Aquarists have not been slow to take advantage of the fertilized eggs' ability to withstand semi-dehydration, and exchange fertile eggs through the post, often on a worldwide basis.

Species may live longer than the expected twelve months under aquarium conditions, where the water never dries up. Other species spawn among aquatic plants, where their environment may not be subject to extreme changes; these species also live longer than twelve months. These fishes are extremely colourful, but they require slightly different conditions from those needed by the usual 'tropical' species. They do not need such a high water temperature and, because of their aggressiveness, are not suitable for a mixed community collection. These species may therefore be kept in smaller quarters (thus in greater numbers of differing species) and aquarists keeping these fishes generally do so to the exclusion of other species. There are specialist Killifish Associations in Britain and the United States.

Killifishes are usually kept in 'peaty' water which has an acid reaction; its amber coloration sets off the colours of the fishes perfectly. They prefer dimly lit aquaria (in nature they follow the shadows around the pool), and this is easily provided by heavily planting the tank; a layer of floating plants will also reduce the amount of light penetrating the water. Most species of Killifishes are cylindrical in body shape, with the mouth situated towards the top of the head. Their natural action is somewhat pike-like: they drift just below the water surface waiting for an opportunity to seize some insect that ventures too near.

63

**Lyretail; Lyre-tailed Panchax;
Cape Lopez Lyretail** *Aphyosemion
australe* 65 mm 2½ in. West Africa,
Gabon: coastal marshes. The cylindrical body is red/brown covered with
dark red speckles. The red dorsal fin
has white extensions, while the anal
fin has a red and green border, with
white extensions. The caudal fin has
yellow edges, with white 'lyretail'
extensions; the centre section is blue,
with red patterning and a dark rear
edge. Females are a paler brown,
without extensions to their fins.
Temperature: 18-22°C (65-72°F).
Diet: insect larvae, worms (fed to the
fish in floating worm feeders), and
dried foods. *Breeding:* removable
nylon mops are used as a spawning
medium by the fishes. Eggs can be
transferred from the mops and stored
in shallow water in plastic dishes
until hatching occurs in two to four
weeks. *Illustrated on previous page.*

Red Lyretail *Aphyosemion bivit-
tatum* 60 mm 2¼ in. West Africa,
Cameroon: streams. The purplish
body has a dark line running from the
snout into the flanks. The scales are
edged in violet or red, giving a
glittering appearance. The ventral,
pectoral and anal fins are red/orange
with blue and red edgings. The dorsal
fin is red/gold, with specklings. The
caudal fin is a mixture of purple,
green and orange, with a blue and
red edge. *Temperature:* 18-22°C
(65-72°F). *Diet:* live and dried foods.
Breeding: mop spawner.

Steel-blue Aphyosemion *Aphyosemion gardneri* 75 mm 3 in. Nigeria,
Cameroon: streams. This species has
several colour variants. The body
colour is blue, with red markings
extending into the fins. The dorsal
and caudal fins have a horizontal red
line parallel to the edge of the fin. The
Blue variety has a white edging to the
fins outside the red line, whereas the
Yellow variety has a yellow margin.
Many 'new' species are often found
to be only regional colour variations
of an already existing species.
Temperature: 18-22°C (65-72°F).
Diet: live and dried foods. *Breeding:*
a ready mop spawner.

Blue Gularis *Aphyosemion sjoe-
stedti* 110 mm 4¼ in. Nigeria, Cameroon: marshy areas. The green-blue/
brown body has a red patch running
from the snout to mid-body. Vertical
red bands cross the rear half of the
body. The anal fin is gold with a blue
and red edging. The dorsal fin has a
red base and red flecking. The large
caudal fin has an orange centre
section extended to the same length
as the outer rays; the upper lobe is
green-blue with a red marking; the
lower lobe is blue with red markings.
Temperature: 18-22°C (65-72°F).
Diet: live and dried foods. *Breeding:*
bottom spawner in peat or non-
floating mops. Eggs may be stored
nearly dry for a month or so before
being re-immersed for hatching to
occur.

Lampeyed Panchax; Lampeye *Ap-
locheilichthys* (formerly *Micropan-
chax*) *macrophthalmus* 30 mm 1¼ in.
Nigeria, Cameroon: forest streams.
The body is not cylindrical, but more
laterally compressed. Its colour is a
delicate blue, with a faint gold line
running from the gill cover to the
caudal fin. The caudal fin may have a
yellow tinge, with red marks at the
edge. The eyes are blue. Unlike some
Killifishes, this species does well in
hard, alkaline water. A shoaling
upper water level species, perhaps
too small for a community collection.
Temperature: 23-26°C (73-78°F).
Diet: live and dried foods. *Breeding:*
lays eggs over period of days in plants
or mops. Eggs hatch in two weeks
and fry mature in six months.

Sabrefin; Sicklefin Killi *Austro-
fundulus dolichopterus* 40 mm 1½ in.
Venezuela: pools. The body colour
varies from violet to red/brown, with
dark speckling over the body and into
the fins. A vertical dark stripe
crosses the eye. The large caudal fin
has extended lobes forming a lyretail.
The dorsal and anal fins are very
elongated. The females have less
exaggerated fins. *Temperature:* 23-
26°C (73-78°F). *Diet:* live and dried
foods. *Breeding:* peat breeder. Eggs
may be rested for five months before
hatching.

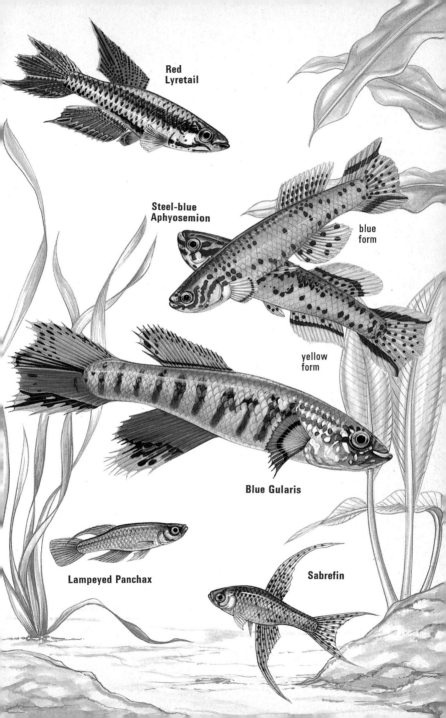

Red
Lyretail

Steel-blue
Aphyosemion

blue
form

yellow
form

Blue Gularis

Lampeyed Panchax

Sabrefin

Striped Panchax

Blue Panchax

Ceylon Killifish

Ceylon Killifish *Aplocheilus dayi* 70 mm 2¾ in. Southern India, Sri Lanka: streams. Has a cylindrical body and pike-like head. The gold-green body has some dark dots on the flanks. The scales appear to be outlined individually. The dorsal fin is set well back and, like the anal fin, may be marked with dark streaks. The caudal fin is round, with a red margin and markings. *Temperature:* 23-26°C (73-78°F). *Diet:* live and dried foods. *Breeding:* may prefer peat fibre as an alternative to mops. Eggs hatch in two weeks.

Striped Panchax *Aplocheilus line-atus* 100 mm 4 in. Southern India, Sri Lanka: streams. Has a golden brown body. The golden scales are redotted on the front half of the body and there are vertical, dark half bands across the rear of the body. The female has broader and more numer-ous dark stripes. The dorsal fin is gold with white dots. The anal fin has a long base with a red edge. The female dorsal fin has a dark spot at the base. The ventral fins are elon-gated in the male. The caudal fin has a red edging along the top and bottom. *Temperature:* 23-26°C (73-78°F). *Diet:* live and dried foods. *Breeding:* mop spawner.

Blue Panchax *Aplocheilus panchax* 75 mm 3 in. India, Sri Lanka, Indo-nesia: still or sluggish waters. The blue body has rows of red dots. The anal fin has a red edging. The dorsal fin is white-tipped and has a dark blotch at its base. The caudal fin is slightly elongated with red speckles and a white edging outlined in black. The colouring of the species is very variable. *Temperature:* 23-26°C (73-78°F). *Diet:* live and dried foods. *Breeding:* mop spawner.

Black-finned Pearl Fish *Cyno-lebias nigripinnis* 50 mm 2 in. Argen-tina, Paraguay, Uruguay: streams. The stocky body and fins are dark grey-black with white dotted mark-ings. The edge of the dorsal and anal fins is white. The female's coloration is almost the opposite — black markings on a light-brown body and fins. The lifespan of this species is very short, perhaps eight months, so young stock should be bought wherever possible. *Temperature:* 22-26°C (72-78°F), but can tolerate lower temperatures in nature. *Diet:* live and dried foods. *Breeding:* buries its eggs, so a peat layer of sufficient depth on the tank floor is essential. Spawning period extends over 8-10 days. Eggs may be stored for three months before hatching.

Rachov's Nothobranch *Nothobranchius rachovi* 50 mm 2 in. East Africa: pools. A very colourful fish, bright-red with light blue specklings. The dorsal and anal fins are blue with red stripes; the caudal fin is blue with red patterning and a black rear edge. The female is quite drab and shows none of her partner's colours. The fish is too aggressive to be kept in a mixed community collection. *Temperature:* 23-26°C (72-79°F). *Diet:* live and dried foods. *Breeding:* buries its eggs. Sometimes female may be too small to spawn. Eggs stored at least six weeks. Fry mature in 6-8 weeks with good feeding.

American Flag Fish *Jordanella floridae* 70 mm 2¾ in. Florida, Yucatán (Mexico): various waters. The stocky, blue-green body has a red, reticulated pattern which extends into the fins of the male. There is also a dark blotch on the flank below the front edge of the dorsal fin. The female does not have red patterning but carries a light-edged dark blotch at the rear edge of the dorsal fin. This fish may be pugnacious. *Temperature:* 18-25°C (65-76°F). *Diet:* live and dried foods. Reputed to eat blue-green algae, and generally appreciates some vegetable matter. *Breeding:* lays eggs in depression in gravel. Male guards eggs and fry; female should be removed after spawning. Author's fish spawned in aquarium plants (*Cabomba*) in midwater, and eggs repeatedly affected by fungus until methylene blue was added to water. Hatching takes 10 days.

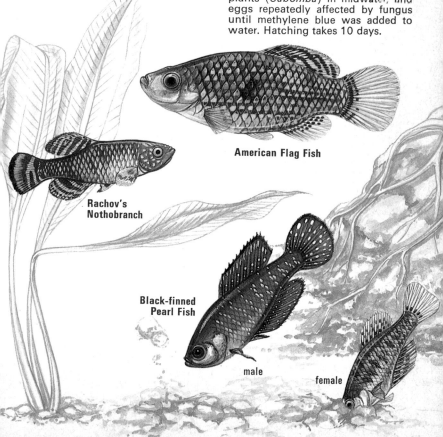

American Flag Fish

Rachov's Nothobranch

Black-finned Pearl Fish

male

female

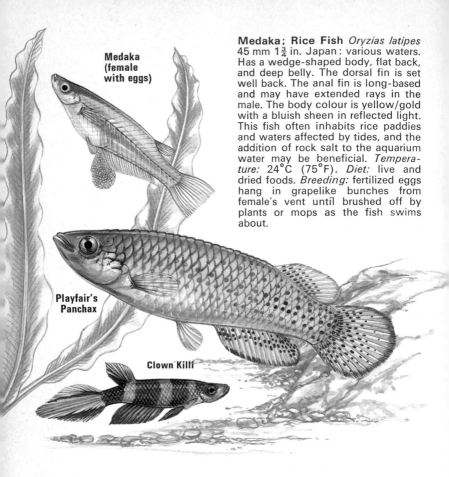

Medaka (female with eggs)

Playfair's Panchax

Clown Killi

Medaka; Rice Fish *Oryzias latipes* 45 mm 1¾ in. Japan : various waters. Has a wedge-shaped body, flat back, and deep belly. The dorsal fin is set well back. The anal fin is long-based and may have extended rays in the male. The body colour is yellow/gold with a bluish sheen in reflected light. This fish often inhabits rice paddies and waters affected by tides, and the addition of rock salt to the aquarium water may be beneficial. *Temperature:* 24°C (75°F). *Diet:* live and dried foods. *Breeding:* fertilized eggs hang in grapelike bunches from female's vent until brushed off by plants or mops as the fish swims about.

Playfair's Panchax *Pachypanchax playfairi* 76 mm 3 in. East Africa, Malagasy, Seychelles :various waters. The cylindrical body is gold-brown with rows of red dots. The fins are blue-yellow with a dark edging and some red dots. The dorsal fin is set well back. A feature of this fish is that the scales are raised, standing out from the body in a manner which suggest the onset of the condition dropsy. *Temperature:* 24°C (75°F). *Diet:* live and dried foods. *Breeding:* mop spawner. Often spawns in a community tank, and the young fry may be rescued from floating plants such as *Riccia* when noticed.

Clown Killi; Rocket Panchax *Pseudoepiplatys annulatus* 45 mm 1¾ in. West Africa: streams. A miniature Killifish, with a light brown cylindrical body ringed by four broad, dark bands. The dorsal fin has bright-red front rays. The caudal fin has an orange-red centre section which extends to a point with light-blue bordering areas. When seen against a dark background the fish may resemble a rocket in flight, hence the common name. This species may be more delicate than other Killifishes. *Temperature:* 24°C (75°F). *Diet:* live and dried foods. *Breeding:* mop spawner. Fry very small.

LIVEBEARING FISHES

Brightly coloured Guppies.

The young of these fishes develop inside the body of the female until they have absorbed the yolk-sac and are then released. Most livebearing fishes are easily sexed: male fishes have the anal fin modified into a rod-like structure called the *gonopodium*, through which the fertilizing spermatophores are introduced into the female. Gestation is approximately 30 days and broods may number from 20 to 200. It is possible for the females of some species to deliver successive broods without a repeat mating with the male.

Such fecundity gives the aquarist plenty of living stock with which to experiment; many colour strains of livebearers seen in dealers are the result of 'line-breeding' programmes by hobbyists, as such colour patternings or fin shapes do not occur in nature. Livebearing fishes are mainly native to Central and South America, but some may be found in Asia. Some species have been introduced into other areas as an aid in the control of malaria – the fishes relish the larvae of the disease-carrying mosquito. Many of these fishes are happy to eat green algae, and some vegetable matter should be regularly provided for them.

In recent years, there has been an upsurge of interest in the livebearing fishes and consequently many more species are being kept, and bred, in aquaria. Many of these species have been classified into one large family, the Poeciliidae, but for ease of reference their former names are also included.

Types of Male Gonopodium

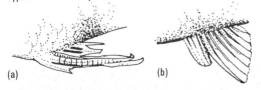

(a) (b)

The majority of livebearing male fishes have gonopodiums as in (a), but fishes in the Goodeidae famile do not have the anal fin so well modified. Their reproductive organ is limited to the first few rays only, as in (b).

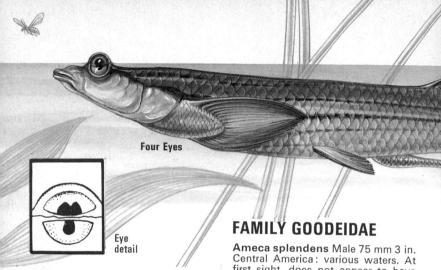

Four Eyes

Eye
detail

FAMILY ANABLEPIDAE

Four Eyes *Anableps anableps*
250 mm 10 in. Central America:
waters near coast. A surface-swim-
ming fish whose eyes protrude
above the water. Each eye is divided
into two halves at the water surface
so that the fish can see above and
below the water at the same time.
The cylindrical body has an olive-
green back with 4 to 5 dark, thin
stripes running along the flanks.
Temperature: 24°C (75°F) or slightly
higher; the addition of some natural
salt to the aquarium water is
beneficial. *Diet:* insect larvae and
floating foods. *Breeding:* may only
be able to mate from one side — that
is, a 'left-handed' male must find a
'right-handed' partner.

FAMILY GOODEIDAE

Ameca splendens Male 75 mm 3 in.
Central America: various waters. At
first sight, does not appear to have
the sexual differences of a livebearing
fish: the anal fin is not completely
modified into a gonopodium; only
the first few rays are slightly separated
from the anal fin to form a primitive
reproductive organ. Has a silvery
blue-grey body covered in dark
brown speckles, which are more
concentrated in a broad band along
the flanks. Males have less distinct
specklings but have a bright yellow
band on the rear edge of the caudal
fin. Species within the Goodeidae
family are often aggressive. *Temperature:* 24°C (75°F). *Diet:* live and dried
foods. *Breeding:* gestation period
may be 6 to 8 weeks. Females cannot
produce successive broods from a
single mating. Young draw nourish-
ment from the female via a placenta
before birth.

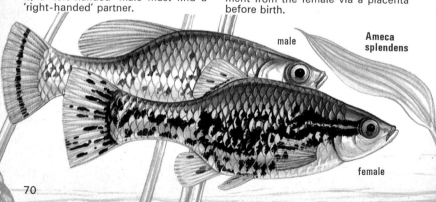

male

**Ameca
splendens**

female

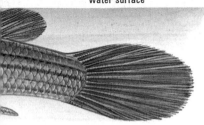

water surface

FAMILY HEMIRHAMPHIDAE

Half Beak; Wrestling Half Beak
Dermogenys pusillus 65 mm 2½ in.
Far East: various waters. Has a long cylindrical body, with the lower jaw extended far beyond the upper, so that the fish is forced to take food from the surface. The anal fin in males is not developed into a rod-like gonopodium but is similar to the fin development in the Goodeidae genera. The aquarium should be well-planted around the glass as the fish, if frightened, may swim into it and damage the lower jaw. A golden brown colour, with some red in the yellow fins. *Temperature:* will tolerate a wide range, from 20-30°C (68-86°F). *Diet:* insects, floating foods. *Breeding:* temperature should be 25°C (76°F) or higher, as low temperatures may result in deformed fry. Females will eat their own young, so shallow water and a well-planted nursery tank essential. Salt may be added to the aquarium but is not vital.

Orange-tailed Goodea *Xenotoca eiseni* Male 65 mm 2½ in; female slightly larger. Central Mexico: various waters. A very colourful fish. The stocky body is metallic turquoise blue, with an orange caudal fin in the male. Females have a silvery yellow body with plain fins. An aggressive fish. *Temperature:* 24°C (75°F). *Diet:* all foods. *Breeding:* prolific, but ratio of males to females in brood may be low.

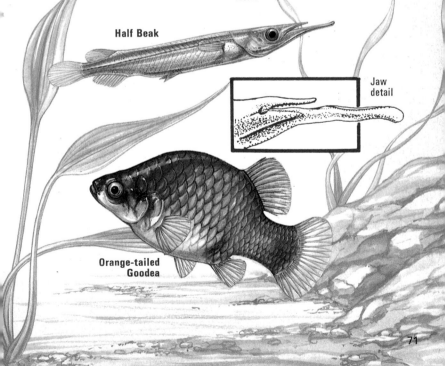

Half Beak

Jaw detail

Orange-tailed Goodea

FAMILY POECILIIDAE

Pike Top Minnow *Belonesox beliz-anus* Male 100 mm 4 in; female 150 mm 6 in. Belize, Guatemala: various waters. A predatory fish which lives up to the reputation of its much larger namesake. The large, tooth-filled mouth and powerful caudal fin bode ill for other fishes in the same tank, full-grown female Guppies being taken with ease. The body is dark blue-green with speckled markings and a spot on the caudal fin base area. *Temperature:* 24°C (75°F). The addition of salt to the water is beneficial. *Diet:* all foods, but predominantly live foods. *Breeding:* usual livebearer pattern.

Eastern Mosquito *Gambusia affinis holbrooki* Male 35 mm $1\frac{1}{4}$ in; female twice as large. Eastern and southern United States: various waters. A popular member of a large genus of some 34 species. The males are small, with quite a large gonopodium, and may become black in colour. The females remain a brown-yellow colour. The dorsal and caudal fins are speckled. Aggressive towards its own species as well as other fishes. *Temperature:* 12-35°C (54-95°F); will live outside in ponds during summer months. *Diet:* all foods, preferably live, but also takes vegetable matter. *Breeding:* females mated too young often miscarry. Fry fairly slow to mature.

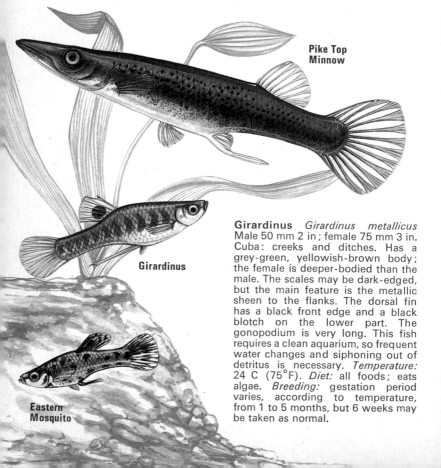

Pike Top Minnow

Girardinus

Eastern Mosquito

Girardinus *Girardinus metallicus* Male 50 mm 2 in; female 75 mm 3 in. Cuba: creeks and ditches. Has a grey-green, yellowish-brown body; the female is deeper-bodied than the male. The scales may be dark-edged, but the main feature is the metallic sheen to the flanks. The dorsal fin has a black front edge and a black blotch on the lower part. The gonopodium is very long. This fish requires a clean aquarium, so frequent water changes and siphoning out of detritus is necessary. *Temperature:* 24 C (75°F). *Diet:* all foods; eats algae. *Breeding:* gestation period varies, according to temperature, from 1 to 5 months, but 6 weeks may be taken as normal.

Pseudo Helleri *Heterandria bimaculata* Male 60 mm $2\frac{1}{4}$ in; female nearly twice as big. Guatemala, Honduras, Mexico: various waters. Although sometimes confused with the Swordtail (*P. xiphophorus*), the male of this species carries no sword. The body may be blue-grey with dark-edged scales and a blue sheen on the flanks. The dorsal fin is yellow with a dark border, and the caudal fin reddish. An aggressive fish not suitable for a community tank. *Temperature:* 25°C (77°F). *Diet:* all foods. *Breeding:* produces numerous fry, but not all at once since the eggs are produced and fertilized continuously.

Mosquitofish; Dwarf Top Minnow; Dwarf Livebearer *Heterandria formosa* Male 20 mm $\frac{3}{4}$ in; female nearly twice as big. Central America: various waters. One of the smallest livebearers and not readily recognized as being related to *H. bimaculata.* The body is brown, with a horizontal dark line and white belly. Some transverse dark bars cross the back down to the horizontal line. The dorsal and anal fins carry dark marks. *Temperature:* 24°C (75°F), or slightly lower. *Diet:* live and dried foods, including vegetable matter. *Breeding:* young produced over a period of days; will eat own young, so a well-planted nursery tank is recommended.

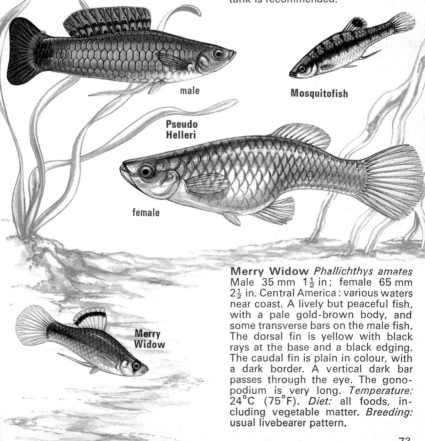

male

Mosquitofish

Pseudo Helleri

female

Merry Widow

Merry Widow *Phallichthys amates* Male 35 mm $1\frac{1}{2}$ in; female 65 mm $2\frac{1}{2}$ in. Central America: various waters near coast. A lively but peaceful fish, with a pale gold-brown body, and some transverse bars on the male fish. The dorsal fin is yellow with black rays at the base and a black edging. The caudal fin is plain in colour, with a dark border. A vertical dark bar passes through the eye. The gonopodium is very long. *Temperature:* 24°C (75°F). *Diet:* all foods, including vegetable matter. *Breeding:* usual livebearer pattern.

73

Guppy; Millions Fish *Poecilia* (formerly *Lebistes*) *reticulata* Male 28-32 mm 1-1¼ in; females 65 mm 2½ in. Trinidad: various waters. A well-known species. No two males are ever exactly alike; the females are much larger and do not share the males' rainbow colours. Genetic experimentation by hobbyists has resulted in many colours and finnage shapes becoming internationally recognized standards. Several specialist groups exist solely for the Guppy fancier. Serious breeders separate the sexes as soon as they are recognizable to prevent unwanted broods. *Temperature:* 24°C (75°F). *Diet:* all foods. *Breeding:* very prolific. Females should be given a separate, well-planted tank in which to give birth.

Blue Limia; Black-bellied Limia *Poecilia* (formerly *Limia*) *melanogaster* Male 45 mm 1¾ in; female 65 mm 2½ in. Jamaica, Haiti: streams. The body colour is silver-blue with several transverse dark stripes. The males are more slender than the females. The female has a large, dark blotch forward of the anal fin, while the male has a dark area which spreads along the ventral contour into the caudal fin. The male's dorsal fin is yellow with a darker band parallel to the rear black edge. The female's dorsal fin lesser coloured. Adult males may have a yellow/orange throat and belly. A peaceful fish. *Temperature:* 24°C (75°F). *Diet:* live and dried foods. *Breeding:* usual pattern.

Humpbacked Limia *Poecilia* (formerly *Limia*) *nigrofasciata* Male 50 mm 2 in; female 70 mm 2¾ in. Haiti: lakes. Has a yellow/brown body with dark-edged scales and several transverse dark stripes. The dorsal fin is speckled. Males have high, arched backs and may become darker with age. The sexes can be identified only when almost full-grown. A peaceful fish. *Temperature:* 24°C (75°F). *Diet:* all foods, including vegetable matter. *Breeding:* usual pattern.

Cuban Limia *Poecilia* (formerly *Limia*) *vittata* Male 57 mm 2¼ in;

female 90 mm 3½ in. Cuba: stream and canals. The body is olive-brown on the back, with shining blue scales on the flanks. Dark speckles are randomly dispersed over the body and into the fins, which are yellow. The belly is silver. *Temperature:* 24°C (75°F). *Diet:* all foods, including vegetable matter. *Breeding:* very prolific; can produce up to 200 young at a time.

Sailfin Molly *Poecilia* (formerly *Mollienisia*) *latipinna* Male 100 mm 4 in; female 110 mm 4½ in. Mexico: various waters, including those affected by tides. The body is olive-green with a yellow overcast; the scales may appear to be iridescent. Several rows of dark dots run along the body, and the belly often has dark transverse bars. The male fish has a very tall dorsal fin. A jet-black variety has been established in the aquarium, and gold and albino strains have become common in recent years. A similar species, *P. velifera* (also known as the Sailfin Molly), grows slightly larger. All Mollies benefit by the addition of salt to the aquarium water. *Temperature:* 24°C (75°F). *Diet:* very fond of greenstuffs, but takes all foods. *Breeding:* usual livebearer pattern, but females become nervous when gravid and should not be moved when about to give birth, otherwise premature births will occur resulting in undeveloped young.

Black Molly; Sphenops Molly *Poecilia* (formerly *Mollienisia*) *mexicana* (*sphenops*) Male 70 mm 2¾ in; female 120 mm 4¾ in. Mexico: various waters, including tidal areas. Wild fishes are greenish silver in colour, but the all-black variety is very popular with aquarists. A midway colour variety, the Speckled Molly, is also found in aquarium circles, as is the Liberty Molly (silver blue with a red dorsal) and various Lyretail strains of the Black and Speckled varieties. *Temperature:* 24°C (75°F); a drop in temperature often brings on 'shimmying' in this species. *Diet:* all foods, especially algae and other green food. *Breeding:* prolific; as with *P. latipinna,* gravid females should be treated with care.

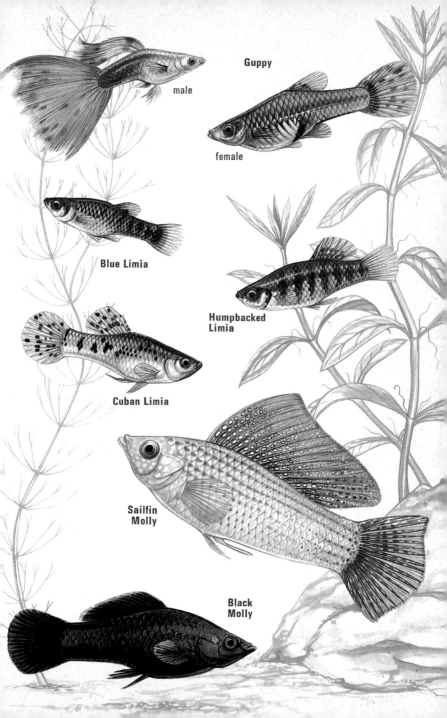

Guppy

male

female

Blue Limia

Humpbacked
Limia

Cuban Limia

Sailfin
Molly

Black
Molly

A pair of Swordtails. The male's sword is green in wild fishes.

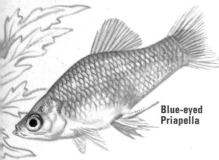

Blue-eyed Priapella

Blue-eyed Priapella *Priapella intermedia* 50 mm 2 in. Mexico: flowing waters. The golden brown body has dark-edged scales. The eyes are bright blue. All the fins are edged with whitish blue when seen against a dark background. A shoaling fish that settles down well and best shows its colours when kept in numbers. Sensitive to water and temperature change. *Temperature:* 24°C (75°F) or slightly higher. *Diet:* all foods. *Breeding:* sexes only distinguishable in mature fishes; gonopodium develops slowly in males. Only a small number of fry in each brood.

Swordtail *Xiphophorus helleri* 100 mm 4 in. Mexico: various waters. An easily recognized species: males have a sword-like extension to the bottom edge of the caudal fin. Females may be slightly deeper in the body and a little longer. Natural species are greenish, with a reddish horizontal stripe and a green sword edged with black. Aquarium varieties include Reds, Red-eyed Reds, Wagtail (coloured body, black fins), Green, Tuxedo and Wiesbaden. These are recognized internationally. Occasionally sex reversal occurs (female to male). *Temperature:* 24°C (75°F). *Diet:* all foods, including vegetable matter. *Breeding:* prolific; broods of over 250 young have been reported.

Platy *Xiphophorus* (formerly *Platypoecilius*) *maculatus* 45-50 mm 2 in. Mexico: various waters. This species is closely related to *X. helleri,* with which it may hybridize, but has a stockier, shorter body than *X. helleri* and no sword. Females may be slightly longer than the males. Again several colour varieties have become standardized in aquarium circles through controlled and selective breeding programmes. *Temperature:* 24°C (75°F). *Diet:* all foods, including vegetable matter. *Breeding:* prolific.

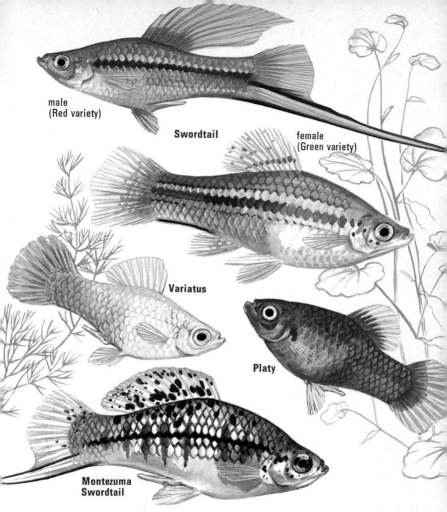

male
(Red variety)

Swordtail

female
(Green variety)

Variatus

Platy

**Montezuma
Swordtail**

Variatus *Xiphophorus* (formerly *Platypoecilius*) *variatus* 57 mm 2½ in. Mexico: various waters. Has a 'stretched' body similar to *X. maculatus.* The scale edges may be dark. Extensive breeding programmes have developed many colour strains including the Marigold and Sunset forms. Aquarium-developed varieties of *X. maculatus* and *X. variatus* have featured exaggerated fins and, in the case of *X. helleri,* double swords. *Temperature:* 24°C (75°F). *Diet:* all foods, including vegetable matter. *Breeding:* prolific.

Montezuma Swordtail *Xiphophorus montezumae* 60 mm 2½ in. Mexico: various waters. A very attractive fish, similar in body shape to *X. helleri* but not so elongated. The pale gold-silver body has dark-edged scales and flanks adorned with blue and black markings. Dark scales along the lateral line link up to form a horizontal line. The sword is not as long as in *X. helleri.* The fins are speckled. *Temperature:* 24°C (75°F). *Diet:* all foods, including vegetable matter. *Breeding:* usual livebearer pattern.

77

LABYRINTH FISHES/FAMILY ANABANTIDAE

Fishes in this family are often referred to as 'labyrinth' fishes because they have a labyrinthine organ in the head which allows them to breathe atmospheric air if necessary. Another distinguishing feature of this group is the breeding pattern: the majority of the fishes are bubblenest builders. The nests are made of saliva-coated bubbles blown by the male, into which the fertilized eggs are placed following the nuptial embrace beneath the nest. The fry are guarded and kept within the vicinity of the nest by the male. The female is best removed after spawning as the male may attack her. When breeding, care should be taken not to allow any cold draughts of air to pass across the water surface as the fry may become chilled. As it is, a fairly high mortality rate occurs within the first two weeks of life with many species, and the ratio of males to females may be low.

Labyrinth fishes are native to Africa and Asia. The Asian species have long, filament-like ventral fins, which can be extended in front of the fish at will. These have taste cells at their tips so that the fish can find food in the often dark waters of its natural habitat. With one or two exceptions, the Anabantidae is a peaceful family and provides welcome additions to the community tank.

bubblenest

Siamese Fighting Fish

male

female

Siamese Fighting Fish *Betta splendens* 60 mm 2¼ in. Thailand : standing waters. This fish has a reputation for the pugnacity of the males, and the likely results of combats between them are the subject of many wagers in their native country. The body is cylindrical, with very flowing fins, particularly the dorsal, anal and caudal fins. The ventral fins are very elongated and narrow. When males confront each other, the gill covers are raised and the fins spread in a threatening manner. The females, which are not aggressive, do not have such elongated fins and are less colourful. Many colour strains exist in the 'man-made' varieties: the Cambodian strain has a light-coloured body with dark-coloured fins. *Temperature:* 24°C (75°F). *Diet:* all foods. *Breeding:* fairly prolific, but space has to be found for the separate accommodation of male fishes from the brood; luckily, in a space-heated fish house, small jars will suffice.

Honey Gourami *Colisa chuna* 45 mm 1¾ in. India: various waters. The smallest of the genus. The body is compressed laterally and is honey-brown in colour. Males have a purple/green coloration to the head and breast, which extends diagonally across the red-edged anal fin during the spawning period. The dorsal fin has a yellow/gold top edge. The ventral fins may be red. The female is a uniform brown, with a dark horizontal stripe along the flanks. *Temperature:* 24°C (75°F). *Diet:* all foods. *Breeding:* fry fairly small and need microscopic first foods — that is, green water and infusoria.

Thick-lipped Gourami *Colisa labiosa* 80 mm 3 in. Burma: various waters. The body is reddish-brown with transverse, slanting stripes of red in the male, blue-green in the female. The fins are bluish, with red edging and patterning in the male, reddish-brown in the female. At breeding time the male changes colour to a dark chocolate with red markings. *Temperature:* 24°C (75°F). *Diet:* all foods. *Breeding:* very prolific.

Dwarf Gourami *Colisa lalia* 60 mm 2½ in. India: various waters. The brilliantly coloured males have a basic body colour of blue/grey overlaid with numerous, zig-zag, slanting, bright-red stripes. The ventral fins are red. The other fins are highly decorated. The females are far less striking in colour. They are grey/brown with only faint turquoise markings and semi-patterned fins. The males are aggressive at breeding time to any other fish in the vicinity. They will also attack the female if she is considered not ready for spawning. *Temperature:* 24°C (75°F). *Diet:* all foods. *Breeding:* bubblenest construction includes pieces of aquatic plants. Male very possessive and protective of nest and fry. Female best removed after spawning. Fry very small, so microscopic food a necessity. Ratio of males to females in brood low.

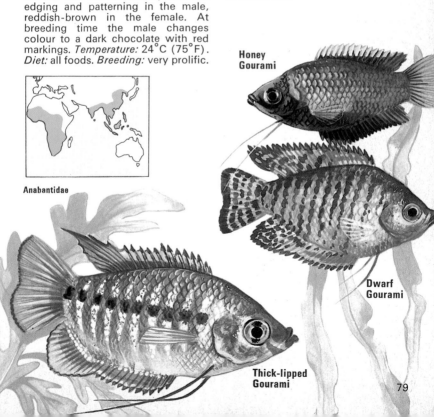

Anabantidae

Honey Gourami

Dwarf Gourami

Thick-lipped Gourami

79

Ctenopoma
kingsleyae

Kissing Gourami

Ctenopoma kingsleyae 200 mm
8 in. Africa: various waters. The
almost oval-shaped body has grey
scales with dark edges. The fins are
also grey with a white edging. Sex
differences are unknown. This species
is usually kept as a specimen fish in
a tank of its own. It appears to be a
sedate fish but may be predatory.
Other species of *Ctenopoma* are
more highly coloured and attractive,
but not commonly available. *Temperature:* 24°C (75°F). *Diet:* all
foods. *Breeding:* some species of
Ctenopoma have been bred in the
aquarium, but details unknown.

Kissing Gourami *Helostoma temmincki* 200 mm 8 in. Far East: various waters. Has a large, pink-coloured body with almost colourless fins. Its main attraction is the 'kissing' action between two fishes using their protruding lips. The real purpose of this lip action in individual fishes is to scrape algae from rocks and other surfaces, but often two fishes approach each other with the well-known amusing result. The action is not a sign of affection, but may be a display of territorial aggression. A green-coloured species, *H. rudolfi*, grows slightly larger. *Temperature:* 24°C (75°F). *Diet:* all foods, particularly greenstuffs. *Breeding:* has been achieved in the aquarium, but is not a regular occurrence. A bubblenest is not built: the eggs float.

Paradise Fish *Macropodus opercularis* 80 mm 3 in. China, Korea, Vietnam: various waters. A very old aquarium favourite introduced in the 1870s. Has a similar body shape to the Gouramis, and is gold/brown with transverse blue bands. The fins are red, blue and brown, with red flecks in the dorsal and caudal fins. Males have elongated fins. An albino form exists in aquarium conditions only. An aggressive fish. *Temperature:* 16-24°C (61-75°F). *Diet:* all foods. *Breeding:* prolific; a bubblenest is built. High temperature (24°C, 75°F) required for breeding.

Gourami *Osphronemus goramy* 500 mm 20 in. Sunda Islands (Indonesia): various waters. A food fish in nature. A grey/pink, mottled fish with a certain appeal to the hobbyist who likes, and can accommodate, big fishes. *Temperature:* 24°C (75°F). *Diet:* consumes large amounts of vegetable matter, such as lettuce, and is usually kept in isolation. *Breeding:* possible, but unlikely to be a regular occurrence in the aquarium.

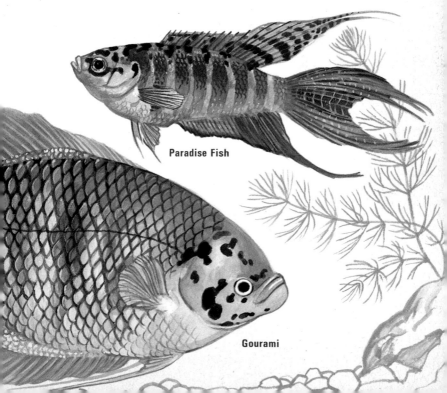

Paradise Fish

Gourami

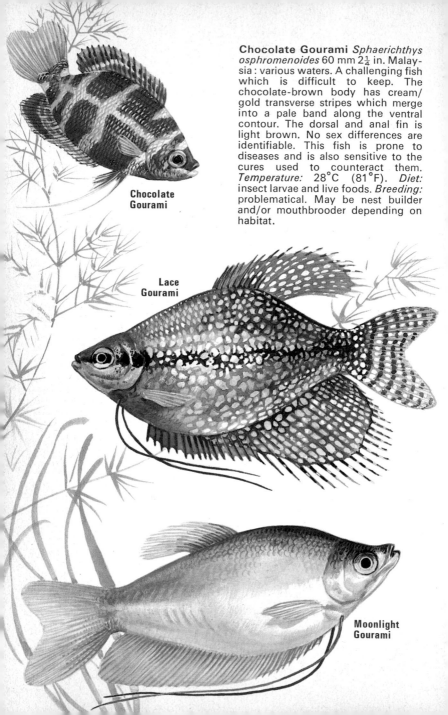

Chocolate Gourami *Sphaerichthys osphromenoides* 60 mm 2¼ in. Malaysia : various waters. A challenging fish which is difficult to keep. The chocolate-brown body has cream/gold transverse stripes which merge into a pale band along the ventral contour. The dorsal and anal fin is light brown. No sex differences are identifiable. This fish is prone to diseases and is also sensitive to the cures used to counteract them. *Temperature:* 28°C (81°F). *Diet:* insect larvae and live foods. *Breeding:* problematical. May be nest builder and/or mouthbrooder depending on habitat.

Chocolate
Gourami

Lace
Gourami

Moonlight
Gourami

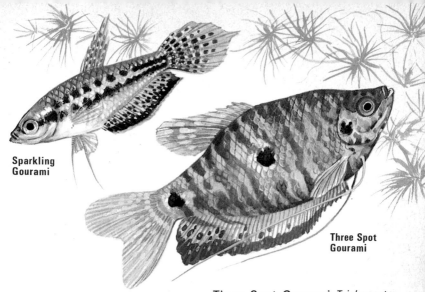

Sparkling Gourami

Three Spot Gourami

Lace, Pearl or **Mosaic Gourami** *Trichogaster leeri* 110 mm 4½ in. Thailand, Malaysia: various waters. A very beautiful fish, whose common name describes it exactly. A mosaic pattern covers the silvery body. The dorsal and anal fins have extended rays in the male. This longer dorsal fin identifies the adult male fish, but develops late as this species does not mature very early. During breeding time the male has an orange throat, breast and part of the anal fin. A dark line runs from the snout along three-quarters of the body. There is a dark spot on the caudal peduncle. The ventral fins are orange. *Temperature:* 24°C (75°F). *Diet:* all foods; will eat *Hydra* if hungry enough. *Breeding:* very prolific, but only spawns when nearly fully grown.

Moonlight Gourami *Trichogaster microlepsis* 140 mm 5½ in. Thailand, Malaysia: various waters. Has a similar body shape to *T. leeri.* The body colour is a burnished silver/grey. The dorsal fin is long in males. The snout is often upturned. A peaceful fish. *Temperature:* 24°C (75°F) or slightly higher. *Diet:* all foods. *Breeding:* prolific.

Three Spot Gourami *Trichogaster trichopterus* 110 mm 4½ in. Thailand, Malaysia, Vietnam: various waters. Has a pale blue/grey body with a central dark spot on the flank, and another on the caudal peduncle. The third 'spot' is formed by the eye. The fins are slightly patterned, and the anal fin is edged with orange. The dorsal fin is longer in the male. Other sub-species include the Blue and Opaline Gouramis. In recent years another variety has been introduced in which the blue coloration is replaced by yellow/gold. This latter form is slightly smaller. *Temperature:* 24°C (75°F). *Diet:* all foods. *Breeding:* prolific.

Sparkling Gourami *Trichopsis* (formerly *Ctenops*) *pumilus* 45 mm 1¾ in. Far East: various waters. A small, beautiful species, with a nearly cylindrical body similar to *B. splendens.* The metallic blue-grey body has dark blotches that form an intermittent horizontal line along the flanks. The fins are yellow/brown with red speckling. The eyes are red. This species emits a croaking sound when mating. A similar species, *T. vittatus,* is a little larger. *Temperature:* 24°C (75°F), or a little higher. *Diet:* all foods. *Breeding:* builds a bubblenest, or may deposit eggs on tank floor.

Cichlid fishes are noted for their care of their young. The Discus takes this care a little further and provides food for its babies in mucus secreted on the parent's body. The Discus is a fish for the more experienced fishkeeper, as it needs special water conditions.

Cichlidae

CICHLIDS/FAMILY CICHLIDAE

These perch-like fishes are considered to be among the more highly evolved species of fishes. The best evidence of this is perhaps the amount of parental care shown by the adult fishes when breeding. A pair of adult fishes will often form a 'pair-bond' which lasts for years. Cichlids are often dismissed as being too aggressive (though some are not), but their various methods of reproduction make them ideal subjects for aquarium study. Breeding methods include laying eggs on open sites, in caves or submerged flowerpots, and incubating fertilized eggs in the female fish's mouth. In all cases, the guarding of the eggs and fry is energetically undertaken. South America has by far the largest natural share of Cichlids, with Africa second; only one genus (with two species) is found in Asia. Generally, the male of the species has the longer fins and the brighter colours, although in some species the female is just as colourful as her mate.

Although usually regarded as omnivorous, and in particular meat-eaters, many Cichlids are not averse to some vegetable matter in their diet. Cichlids are quite happy at normal tropical aquarium temperatures (24°C, 75°F), and with the chemistry of the water from the domestic supply. They can be most rewarding, but there are a few challenging species that need special treatment and aquarium conditions.

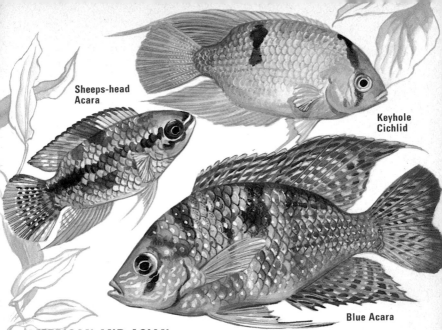

Sheeps-head Acara

Keyhole Cichlid

Blue Acara

AMERICAN AND ASIAN CICHLIDS

The species in this group live in a wide range of natural habitats in rivers and lakes. They include many aquarium favourites, such as the Blue Acara, the Angelfish and the Oscar. Most are fairly large and may be aggressive at times.

Keyhole Cichlid *Aequidens maronii* 100 mm 4 in. Guyana, Surinam, French Guiana: rivers. Not a very colourful fish, the body colour varying from cream to dark brown. The main characteristic is the keyhole-shaped blotch on the flanks, which is quite recognizable in young specimens but tends to spread into a less distinct pattern with maturity. A dark, oblique stripe runs through the eye. A peaceful, even shy fish, which can live to over seven years in the aquarium. *Temperature:* 24°C (75°F). *Diet:* all foods. *Breeding:* not difficult, but fry may be harder to raise than those of other *Aequidens* species.

Sheeps-head Acara; Flag Cichlid *Aequidens curviceps* 75 mm 3 in. South America, Amazon basin: rivers. The grey-green body is slightly iridescent under reflected light. The scales have dark edges, the fins are flecked with blue-green and the dorsal fin is blue-edged. A peaceful fish. *Temperature:* 24°C (75°F). *Diet:* all foods. *Breeding:* deposits eggs on an open site. Parents often eat their first spawning but, given a tank to themselves, usually prove to be good parents subsequently.

Blue Acara *Aequidens pulcher* (formerly *latifrons*) 180 mm 7 in. Venezuela, Colombia, Panama: rivers. An old-established aquarium favourite. A larger Cichlid, similar in coloration to *A. curviceps*, but with more blue streaking over the head and speckling over the body and fins. Some dark patches may be evident under the eyes and on the flanks and caudal peduncle. Fairly pugnacious; may eat small fishes such as Neon Tetras. *Temperature:* 24°C (75°F). *Diet:* all foods. *Breeding:* very prolific; may damage plants when preparing a spawning site. Good parents.

Oscar *Astronotus ocellatus* 300 mm 12 in. South America, widely distributed. A large fish whose adult coloration is quite different from its juvenile form. The black and white, marbled colour of the young turns to an olive-brown, mottled with red speckles and rust-coloured patches. The head is blunt and the mouth very large. A gold-edged, black blotch is present on the caudal peduncle. The attraction of the adult fish is that it becomes very tame: it takes food from its owner's hands and is reputed even to enjoy a friendly stroke. Needs a large tank. *Temperature:* 24°C (75°F). *Diet:* a hearty eater of meaty foods, but will eat almost anything. Because of its large appetite, the tank soon soon becomes dirty with the fish's droppings and partial changes of water should be done frequently. *Breeding:* very prolific.

Festive Cichlid; Flag Cichlid *Cichlasoma festivum* 150 mm 6 in. Amazon basin. A peaceful, often shy fish. It has a yellow-green body with silvery flanks, over which a number of dark, vertical bars may be apparent. A dark stripe runs from the snout through the eye and diagonally upwards to the rear point of the dorsal fin. There is a dark spot on the caudal peduncle. The ventral fins are long and very slender, similar to those of the Angelfish, whose company it often shares in its native habitat. It prefers a quiet tank with not too many boisterous fish for company. It can be very beautiful when kept in a shoal. *Temperature:* 24°C (75°F). *Diet:* all foods. *Breeding:* reported to be problematical, perhaps because the fishes do not select a mate as readily as other species. The eggs are often left unguarded or even eaten, and should therefore be transferred to a separate tank for artificial hatching.

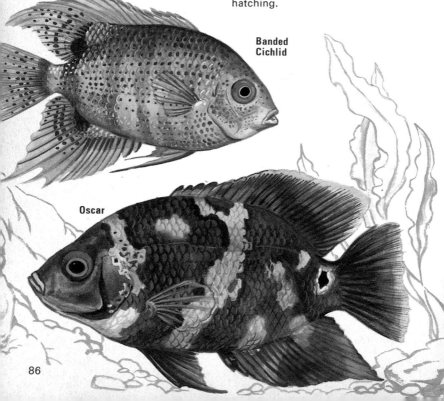

Banded Cichlid

Oscar

Firemouth *Cichlasoma meeki* 150 mm 6 in. Central America (Guatemala, Yucatán). The head of this species is pointed, with a steep forehead. The body is deep and laterally compressed. A gold-edged black spot is present on the gill cover, and a black patch occurs on the flank below the dorsal fin. Some dark, vertical bars may be present depending on the fish's mood. The dorsal fin may be elongated into filaments in the male. The male's throat and belly region is crimson red, and this is intensified in the breeding period. This fish may be guilty of occasional digging, but is generally peaceful and less shy than *C. festivum*. *Temperature:* 24°C (75°F). *Diet:* all foods. *Breeding:* fairly prolific.

Banded Cichlid *Cichlasoma severum* 20 mm 8 in. Central America and Amazon basin. A stocky, deep-bodied fish, green-brown in colour. Young specimens have several vertical, dark bands crossing the body, but these fade with maturity. Adult fishes have a dark, vertical band connecting the rear edges of the dorsal and anal fins across the caudal peduncle. The flanks are patterned with red dots. Recently, a gold form has been introduced to the hobby. Generally a peaceful fish, but it turns aggressive at breeding time. *Temperature:* 24°C (75°F). *Diet:* all foods. *Breeding:* fairly prolific, especially from naturally selected parents.

Pike Cichlid *Crenicichla lepidota* 230 mm 9 in. Central America : various waters. A predatory fish, with a pointed head and large mouth. The powerfully built, torpedo-shaped body is blue-grey with a speckling of silver-white dots. A dark line runs from the snout horizontally along the body to a light-ringed dark spot in the caudal fin. This fish cannot be kept with other fishes, and is even aggressive towards its own kind. The tank should be large enough to accommodate rocky hiding places. *Temperature:* 24°C (75°F). *Diet:* a voracious feeder, all foods being literally snapped up. *Breeding:* deposits eggs in pits in the gravel and guards them.

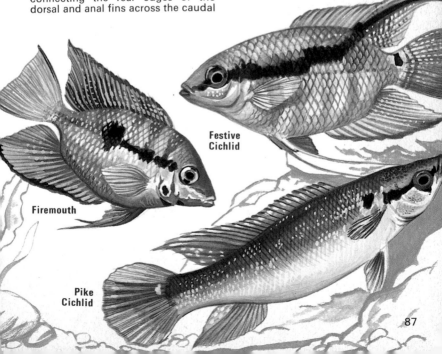

Festive
Cichlid

Firemouth

Pike
Cichlid

Orange Chromide *Etroplus macu-latus* 90 mm 3½ in. India, Sri Lanka: fresh and brackish waters. A peaceful, colourful Cichlid from Asia, which contributes only this one genus to the hobby. The body colour is deep gold, with rows of red dots on the flanks. A large, black area on the lower flanks is surmounted by a series of dark, oval dots. The anal fin has a black area at the front; the ventral fins are dark. The eyes are dark with a red iris and blue scales beneath. The related Silver (or Green) Chromide, *E. suratensis,* is a much larger fish (300 mm 12 in.) and is dark coloured with silver specklings. Both species appreciate the addition of some salt to the water. *Temperature:* 24°C (75°F). *Diet:* all foods. *Breeding:* lays dark-coloured eggs. Young attached to spawning site by sticky threads and often attach themselves to the adults' bodies before free swimming.

Earth Eater; Devil Fish *Geophagus jurupari* 230 mm 9 in. Brazil: various waters. The green-yellow body is covered in pearly scales. The tri-angular-shaped head has a high, sloping forehead and high-set eyes. Has a habit of sifting gravel through its mouth for food and expelling the residue out from the gills. Furnishings in the tank should be able to with-stand such treatment. Fairly terri-torially minded, but really quite peaceful. *Temperature:* 24°C (75°F). *Diet:* all foods. *Breeding:* mouth-brooder; eggs incubated in mouth of female for about two weeks. Male should be removed from breeding tank when fry emerge.

Angelfish *Pterophyllum scalare* (*eimekei*) 110 mm 4½ in. Amazon basin. Perhaps the most widely recognized aquarium fish, apart from the Goldfish. The disc-shaped body is very compressed laterally. The high dorsal fin is equally matched by the long anal fin. The caudal fin is triangular, and the ventral fins have elongated, bony rays. A slow-moving, graceful fish. Colour varieties include the original natural silver fish with four black vertical dark bars; and the aquarium-developed All-Black, Half-Black, Marbled, Blushing and Gold varieties. Similarly, the finnage has been further developed into Lace and Veiltail forms. This fish appreciates deep tanks and tall, grass-like plants such as *Vallisneria* and *Sagittaria*, among which it can glide. Usually peaceful until large, when small, colourful fishes might be regarded as a likely meal. *Temperature:* 24°C (75°F), slightly higher for breeding. *Diet:* all foods, especially insect larvae. *Breeding:* deposits eggs on near-vertical surfaces which are pre-cleaned. Sites may be plant leaves or pieces of slate. Eggs are fanned, guarded and moved to newer, pre-pared sites until hatching occurs.

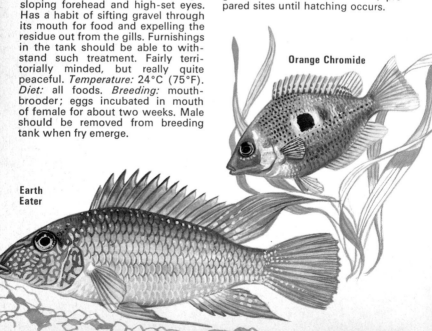

Orange Chromide

Earth Eater

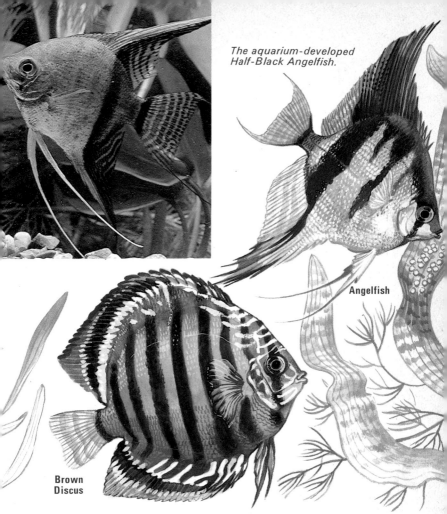

The aquarium-developed Half-Black Angelfish.

Angelfish

Brown Discus

Brown Discus; Pompadour Fish
Symphysodon aequifasciata axelrodi
150 mm 6 in. Amazon basin. A slow-moving and graceful fish with a disc-shaped body and dorsal and anal fins that follow the body contour. The body colour is brown, with eight or nine dark, vertical bands crossing the body. Blue-green wavy lines cover the head, dorsal and anal fins. The dorsal and anal fins also have a dark band running through them, following the outline of the body. The edges of these fins and the ventral fins are red. This genus is very demanding in its requirements: soft water, regular replacement of a proportion with water of similar composition, and high temperature. *Temperature:* 28-32°C (82-91°F). *Diet:* live foods; beef heart and some dried foods taken. *Breeding:* spawns in similar manner to the Angelfish; fry, when free swimming, feed from special mucus developed on parents' bodies; it is consequently very difficult to raise the young away from the adult fishes.

AFRICAN CICHLIDS

The majority of African Cichlids inhabit the Rift Valley lakes and are spectacularly coloured. These fishes are from naturally hard waters, unlike their South American relatives, and many relish algae or other vegetable matter in their diet. Some are mouthbrooding, and all appreciate a tank furnished with hideaways.

Aulonacara nyassae 150 mm 6 in. Lakes Malawi (Nyasa) and Tanganyika. Has an elongated, fairly deep body. Young males and females have brown bodies with several vertical dark bars, but mature males are deep royal blue with a red/gold suffusion on the flanks, which are crossed with dark bars. The fins are blue; the dorsal fin is edged with pale blue and the caudal fin has dark blue/black streaks. A peaceful fish, but caves and hiding places must be provided in a reasonably sized tank. *Temperature:* 24°C (75°F). *Diet:* all foods. *Breeding:* mouthbrooder.

Haplochromis burtoni 130 mm 5 in. Lake Tanganyika and local rivers. The fairly deep and laterally compressed body is typical of the genus, which contains nearly 150 species. The body colour is yellow/grey, with blue areas forming vertical bands on the flanks. Two black lines cross the snout, and a dark band runs diagonally through the eye. The top of the gill cover has a dark patch, and there is a diffuse red area immediately behind the gill opening. The fins are speckled with red. The dorsal fin has a red edge. The anal fin has 4 to 5 dark-ringed, red or yellow spots. *Temperature:* 24°C (75°F). *Diet:* all foods. *Breeding:* mouthbrooder. The female picks up the eggs immediately after laying them in a depression in the gravel. She then attempts to pick up the 'egg-spots' on the male's anal fin and in doing so may stimulate the release of fertilizing milt. This is then drawn into her mouth to complete the fertilization of the eggs. Males take no part in brood care and may be removed from the breeding tank. During the incubation period the female takes no food and becomes quite thin. The fry regard the female's mouth as a safe refuge after free swimming and return there when danger threatens.

Aulonacara
nyassae

Leopard Cichlid *Haplochromis poly-stigma* 230 mm 9 in. Lake Malawi (Nyasa). Has the typical *Haplochromis* body shape, but with a most striking coloration. The body colour is cream, with brown patches overlaid with a speckling of smaller, brown dots. All the fins carry this patterning, although that on the anal fin again represents 'egg-spots'. *Temperature:* 24°C (75°F). *Diet:* all foods. *Breeding:* as for *H. burtoni.*

Jewel Cichlid *Hemichromis bimaculatus* 120 mm 4¾ in. Throughout Africa. An aggressive fish, whose behaviour is redeemed by its brilliant coloration and exceptional conduct as a parent. The reddish-brown body has an overlay of shining blue-green speckles. There is a black spot midway along the flanks and another on the gill cover. The fins are also speckled. At breeding time both sexes change to a brilliant red colour. This species has often been used in laboratory tests to evaluate fish intellect. *Temperature:* 24°C (75°F). *Diet:* all foods. *Breeding:* usual Cichlid pattern; open site spawner.

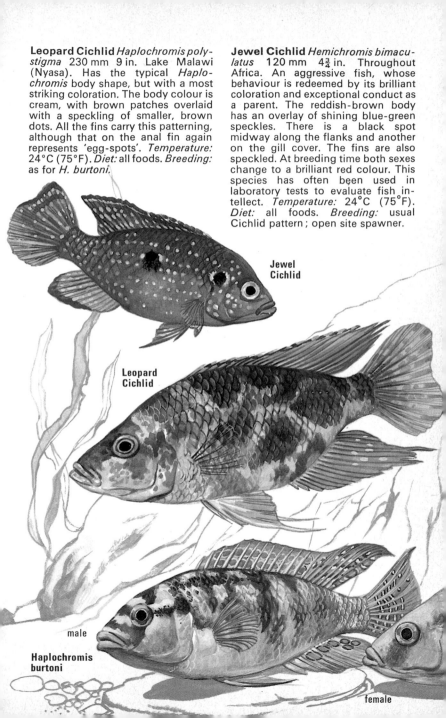

Jewel Cichlid

Leopard Cichlid

male

Haplochromis burtoni

female

Marlier's Julie

Julie

Marlier's Julie *Julidochromis marlieri* 110 mm 4½ in. A very smart-looking fish with a cylindrical, cream body with dark markings that link up to form a latticed pattern. The long-based dorsal fin has light blue edging and flecking. The light blue anal fin has a dark edge. The caudal fin is rounded and has a dark edge bordered with light blue. Hard water must be provided, with rocky retreats. *Temperature:* 24°C (75°F). *Diet:* all foods, including algae and lettuce. *Breeding:* deposits eggs on inside roof of cave or on undersides of rocks.

Julie *Julidochromis ornatus* 80 mm 3¼ in. Lake Tanganyika. The yellow body has three dark, horizontal bands. There is a dark spot at the base of the yellow caudal fin, which has a dark edge. The dorsal and anal fins are yellow, with black and light-coloured edgings. *Temperature:* 24°C (75°F). *Diet* and *Breeding:* as for *J. marlieri.*

Fuelleborn's Cichlid *Labeotropheus fuelleborni* 180 mm 7 in. Lake Malawi (Nyasa). The elongated, blue body has several darker blue, vertical bands. Two dark bands cross the snout. All the fins, except the pectorals, have red areas, and the anal fin carries 2 to 4 oval, dark-edged yellow spots. There is a dark mark immediately behind the gill opening. Females are generally blue, but some are orange, peppered with black dots and blotches. The mouth is somewhat underslung, as this species browses on algae-covered surfaces. *Temperature:* 24°C (75°F). *Diet:* all foods, including greenstuffs. *Breeding:* mouthbrooder.

Red-finned Cichlid; Red Top Zebra *Labeotropheus trewavasae.* 150 mm 6 in. Lake Malawi (Nyasa). The body is blue, with darker, vertical bands. The dorsal fin is bright red/orange. The caudal fin has some red speckling, and the anal fin bears 2 to 3 yellow spots. Females are usually blue, but speckled versions occur as in *L. fuelleborni. Temperature:* 24°C (75°F). *Diet* and *Breeding:* as for *L. fuelleborni.*

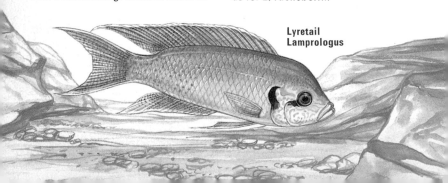

Lyretail Lamprologus

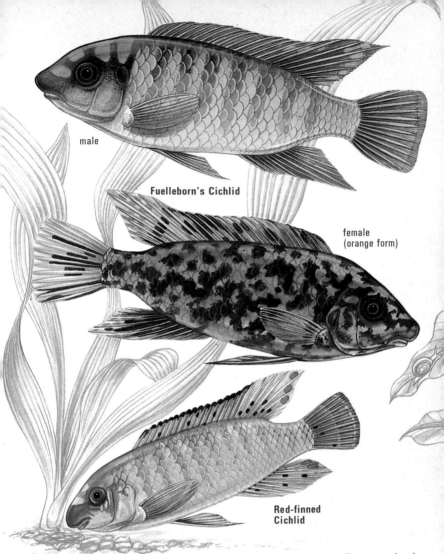

male

Fuelleborn's Cichlid

female
(orange form)

Red-finned
Cichlid

Lyretail Lamprologus *Lamprologus brichardi* (formerly *Lamprologus savoryi elongatus*) 100 mm 4 in. Lake Tanganyika. A very beautiful fish, with a grey/light brown body and dark-edged scales. The gill cover carries a dark stripe, above which is a gold spot. Blue lines adorn the cheek and the blue eye is crossed with a horizontal dark line extending into the gill cover. All the fins are edged with light blue/white. The caudal fin is lyre-shaped, with extended outer rays. The ventral fins have white extensions. The dorsal and anal fins are elongated in the male. This fish appreciates rocky retreats. *Temperature:* 24°C (75°F). *Diet:* all foods. *Breeding:* secretive; deposits eggs on walls or roofs of caves. Parental care exercised.

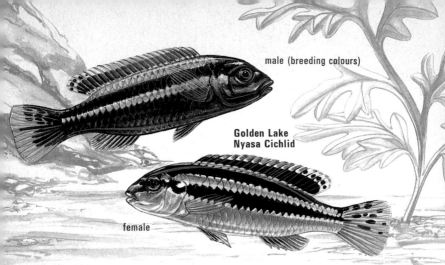

male (breeding colours)

**Golden Lake
Nyasa Cichlid**

female

Golden Lake Nyasa Cichlid *Mela-nochromis* (formerly *Pseudotropheus*) *auratus* 100 mm 4 in. Lake Malawi (Nyasa). Has an elongated, bright-yellow body. Two black bands, edged on either side with white, run along the back from the snout to the base of the caudal fin. The dorsal and caudal fins have black patterning; the anal fin is plain yellow. During the breeding period, the male changes from yellow to blue/black, and the horizontal bands become yellow, edged with white. The dorsal fin turns to light yellow/blue; the caudal fin becomes dark with a yellow edge, and the anal fin dark with a white edge. This fish may be aggressive and should be given a large tank with many hiding places. *Temperature:* 24°C (75°F). *Diet:* all foods, including vegetable matter. *Breeding:* mouth-brooder.

Zebra Nyasa Cichlid *Pseudotro-pheus zebra* 150 mm 6 in. Lake Malawi (Nyasa). The body colour is light blue. The head is a dark blue-black, crossed with two light blue bands. The gill cover has blue patches. Several dark blue, vertical bands cross the body rearwards of the gill opening. The dorsal and anal fins carry yellow dots on their trailing edges. The ventral fins are dark with light blue first rays. *Temperature:* 24°C (75°F). *Diet* and *Breeding:* as for *Melanochromis auratus*.

African Blockhead Cichlid *Steato-cranus casuarius* 100 mm 4 in. Zaire River: rapids and waterfalls. This sombrely coloured fish has a brown-grey body with few other markings, apart from light-edged scales. The characteristic feature is the hump on the forehead, which is more developed in the male. Although aggressive, it is not an active fish and remains in rocky crevices, which should be provided in the aquarium. *Temperature:* 24°C (75°F). *Diet:* live foods. *Breeding:* cave or flowerpot spawner; often pre-chews food for its fry, and digs retreats for them.

**Mozambique
Cichlid**

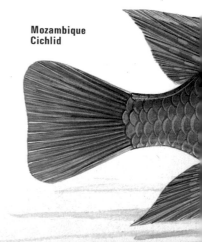

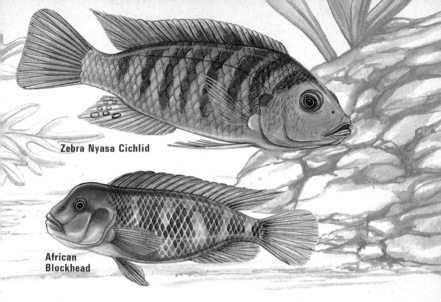

Zebra Nyasa Cichlid

African Blockhead

Mozambique Cichlid *Sarotherodon mossambicus* (formerly *Tilapia mossambica*) 350 mm 13 in. East Africa. The genera *Sarotherodon* and *Tilapia* contain the largest African Cichlids, and many are too large for the aquarium, being normally caught for food. *S. mossambicus* is a heavily built fish with a large mouth. Of variable colour, usually grey-brown, it undergoes a transformation at breeding time. It becomes almost jet black,

with the lower jaw and gill cover remaining white. The lips and snout are light blue. The dorsal and caudal fins are black, edged in bright crimson. The pectoral fins may be red-tinged. This species is noted for its digging activity and should be housed in a large aquarium. *Temperature:* 24°C (75°F). *Diet:* a greedy fish, taking all foods. *Breeding:* a mouthbrooder, but breeding hardly practicable in domestic aquaria.

DWARF CICHLIDS

A number of American and African Cichlids are smaller and less aggressive than the larger Cichlids, and are suitable for the community tank.

Agassiz's Dwarf Cichlid *Apistogramma agassizi* 70 mm 2¾ in. Amazon basin: shady streams. The elongated body is brown, with a blue sheen in the male and dark-edged scales. The caudal fin of the male is spear-shaped, with a white outline inside the dark margin. The long-based dorsal fin is edged in red and white. Females are more drab, with a yellow-brown body that has a dark, horizontal line running along the flanks and a slanting, dark line through the eye. The caudal fin is rounded. In general, females of the *Apistogramma* genus (except for the following species) are similar and difficult to identify. *Temperature:* 24°C (75°F), or slightly higher. *Diet:* all foods. *Breeding:* secretive; deposits eggs in caves or upturned flowerpots.

Ram; Dwarf Butterfly Cichlid *Papillochromis ramirezi* (formerly *Apistogramma ramirezi* or *Microgeophagus ramirezi*) 70 mm 2¾ in. Venezuela: streams. The body colour is blue-green-gold, covered in iridescent speckles — a very spectacular fish in reflected light. There are several dark blotches on the flanks, and the belly may be violet-pink. Red and blue lines appear on the head. The first rays of the dorsal and ventral fins are black. The second ray of the male's dorsal fin is usually elongated. A dark, vertical bar passes through the eye. A gold variety has recently been introduced, but it retains some purple coloration on the flanks in addition to the iridescent scales. A somewhat shy fish often hiding in plant thickets. It prefers soft water, but can become acclimatized to hard water by gradual substitution during partial water changes, or by the natural hardening of the water by the aquarium gravel. *Temperature:* 24°C (75°F), or slightly higher. *Diet:* all foods. *Breeding:* digs pits in which to deposit eggs; may eat first spawn, but usually good parents subsequently.

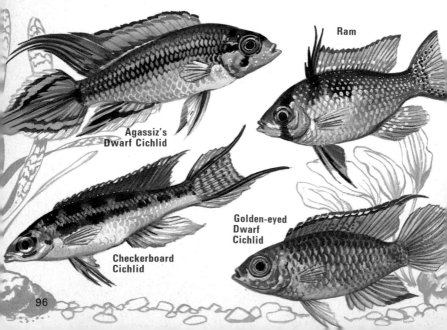

Ram

Agassiz's
Dwarf Cichlid

Checkerboard
Cichlid

Golden-eyed
Dwarf
Cichlid

Checkerboard Cichlid *Crenicara filamentosa* 75 mm 3 in. Amazon basin: shady streams. The elongated and cylindrical body is gold-green in colour, with black blotches giving a checkerboard pattern. The outer rays of the caudal fins are extended into filaments; the fins are more elongated in the male. A similar species. *C. maculata,* does not have the filaments on the fins. A rather shy fish that tends to creep around the base of the aquarium. It is sensitive to water conditions, so a clean tank is necessary. *Temperature:* 24°C (75°F). *Diet:* all foods, particularly worms. *Breeding:* deposits eggs in prepared sites or in crevices.

Golden-eyed Dwarf Cichlid *Nannacara anomala* 70 mm 2¾ in. Guyana. The brown body has a greenish sheen under reflected light. The dorsal fin is long-based and edged with red and white. There is some dark patterning on the head and gill covers, and dark, vertical bars may appear on the flanks if the fish is excited or frightened. The slightly smaller female normally has dark, horizontal stripes, but extra transverse bars may appear, depending on the fish's mood, or during breeding. The eyes are golden red. A similar species, *N. taenia,* is more heavily marked with a dark, lattice-work patterning. *Temperature:* 24°C (75°F). *Diet:* live and dried foods; relishes worms of suitable size. *Breeding:* uses flowerpots, or may excavate its own preferred site. The female guards the eggs and fry and may attack the male, which should be removed after spawning.

Kribensis *Pelvicachromis* (formerly *Pelmatochromis*) *pulcher* 100 mm 4 in. Cameroon: various waters. A favourite among aquarists. The body colour is brown, with a blue/violet overcast and a purple belly region that becomes intensely coloured at breeding time. The dorsal fin is gold-edged, and that of the female has a dark spot at the rear edge. The male's caudal fin is spear-shaped and has a number of dark, round dots in the upper half. The female's caudal fin is rounded. These fishes are great diggers, re-arranging the gravel in the tank to their liking. Undergravel filters (unless protected by a mesh under the gravel) will not function properly if uncovered by digging fishes, and other methods of filtration should be employed. *Temperature:* 24°C (75°F). *Diet:* all foods.*Breeding:* secretive; uses flowerpots, or digs under rocks to prepare site for eggs. Not uncommon for two adult fish to disappear from regular view for a week or two, and then to reappear with 30-40 young fry. Brood invariably includes a predominance of one sex; some sources advocate altering the water chemistry to redress the balance in later spawnings.

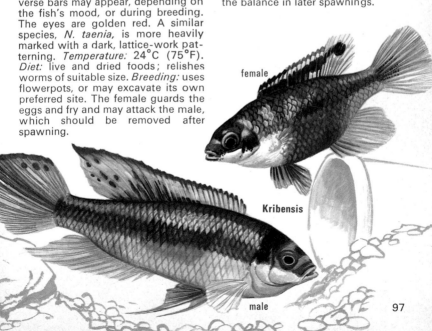

female

Kribensis

male

97

Badis

South American Leaf Fish

Nandidae

FAMILY NANDIDAE

Species of this family are native to South America, Africa, India, Burma, Thailand and Indonesia. Most are aggressive and predatory, but their colours and behaviour ensure their popularity.

Badis; Dwarf Chameleon Fish
Badis badis 65 mm 2½ in. India: standing waters. This fish can change its body colours and patterning to suit its surroundings. Generally it is a dark reddish-brown, with a greenish sheen. From time to time transverse bars may appear. The dorsal fin (similar in shape to that of Dwarf Cichlids) and caudal fin are greenish. The female fish is less colourful. This species is not so aggressive as the rest of the family; it may be kept in the community tank, which should be heavily planted and have many hiding places. *Temperature:* 24°C (75°F). *Diet:* all foods, particularly meat and small worms. *Breeding:* spawns in caves and flowerpots, like the Dwarf Cichlids.

South American Leaf Fish *Polycentrus schomburgki* 90 mm 3½ in. North-eastern South America: standing waters. A stealthy, predatory fish that can swallow fishes of nearly its own length with its protrudable mouth. Its oval, pointed body (resembling a dead leaf) is light brown with dark dots. The fins are clear. At breeding time, the male turns almost black, with a cream line running from the snout to the caudal fin along the top edge of the body. *Temperature:* 24°C (75°F). *Diet:* all foods, in copious amounts. *Breeding:* eggs laid on the ceiling of caves or in flowerpots. Male fish guards the eggs; the female is best removed after spawning.

Australian Rainbow Fish

Celebes Rainbow Fish

RAINBOWFISHES AND SILVERSIDES/ FAMILY ATHERINIDAE

The fishes in this group are related to the Mullets of the oceans. A characteristic feature is the possession of two separate dorsal fins.

Madagascar Rainbow *Bedotia geayi* 100 mm 4 in. Malagasy: various waters. The elongated body is a light golden-brown colour. Two dark, slightly iridescent bands appear on the flanks; one runs from the snout to the caudal fin (into which it extends for a short distance), another from behind the gills along the belly to the rear end of the anal fin. The second dorsal is long-based. The caudal is black-edged, and the male fish has red areas outside the black. A shoaling fish. *Temperature:* 24°C (75°F). *Diet:* all foods, but insect larvae particularly relished. *Breeding:* eggs are laid over a period of days in nylon mops, from which they may be transferred to a separate hatching tank. The fry will accept newly hatched Brine Shrimps immediately, but all foods must be circulated throughout the tank by aeration as the fry only feed at the surface.

Australian Rainbow Fish; Dwarf Rainbow Fish; Black-lined Rainbow Fish *Melanotaenia maccullochi* 90 mm 3½ in. North-eastern Australia: running waters. The elongated, deep body is a silvery-blue colour, with horizontal rows of red-brown dots. A red blotch appears on the gill cover. The second dorsal fin and the anal fin are greenish at the base, turning to red with a yellow edge. The caudal fin may be red. The male fish has a reddish-gold blush to the body, which may be intense on the chest area during breeding time. These are shoaling fishes which appreciate adequate swimming space and some sunshine reaching their tank. *Temperature:* 24°C (75°F). *Diet:* all foods. *Breeding:* eggs may be laid over a period of days; being adhesive, they lodge in the plants. Adult fishes do not eat the eggs, which hatch in 7 to 10 days.

Celebes Rainbow Fish *Telmatherina ladigesi* 70 mm 2¾ in. Celebes, Borneo: various waters. The elongated body is light yellow, and a light-blue, glowing line runs horizontally along the rear half. The second dorsal and the anal fin are large, with black first rays. The male fish has filamentous extensions to these fins which give the fish a rather tattered look. The caudal fin is almost lyre-shaped, with white edging. This fish prefers hard water. *Temperature:* 24°C (75°F). *Diet:* all foods. *Breeding:* spawning mops may be used. The fry need very fine first food.

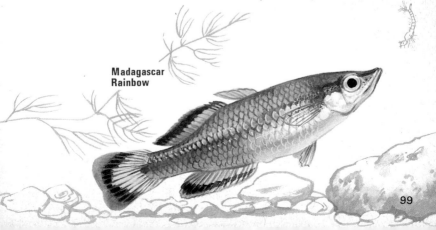

Madagascar Rainbow

MISCELLANEOUS SPECIES

The following fishes, whilst not so widely kept as the foregoing genera, may be encountered occasionally. Several have unusual body shapes or swimming characteristics; others have developed highly sophisticated navigational aids.

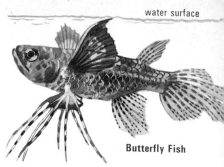

water surface

Butterfly Fish

Fire Eel *Mastacembelus erythrotaenia* 66 mm 27 in. Thailand : various waters. A large, exotic example from the Spiny Eel family (Mastacembelidae). Other, smaller species of the genus are often finely marked and spend most of the time buried in the gravel with only the head protruding. *Temperature:* 24°C (75°F). *Diet:* worms and meat-based foods. *Breeding:* some species of *Mastacembelus* have bred in the aquarium, but no details available.

Butterfly Fish *Pantodon bucholzi* 110 mm 4 in. West Africa: still waters. The only species in the Family Pantodontidae, *P. bucholzi* is a surface-dwelling fish with well-developed pectoral fins resembling outspread butterfly wings when viewed from above. A great jumper. *Temperature:* 25-30°C (76-86°F). *Diet:* live foods, such as crickets and beetles. *Breeding:* the fertilized eggs float, and the fry need tiny insects as first food.

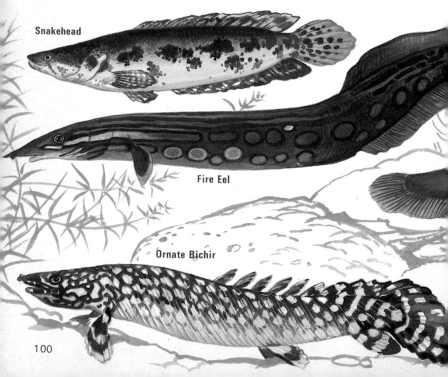

Snakehead

Fire Eel

Ornate Bichir

Snakehead *Ophicephalus obscurus* 300 mm 12 in. Africa: widely distributed. This predatory fish from the Ophicephalidae family is also an excellent jumper, and its tank should be securely covered. *Temperature:* 24°C (75°F). *Diet:* worms, meat foods and young fishes. *Breeding:* the eggs float and the male guards them.

Ornate Bichir *Polypterus ornatipinnis* 450 mm 16 in. Africa (Zaire region): rivers. The Family Polypteridae contains primitive fishes which can survive out of water. The dorsal fin is made up of a number of tiny finlets, and the fish often rests propped up on its pectoral fins. Mainly nocturnal and peaceful. *Temperature:* 24°C (75°F). *Diet:* worms, maggots and other live foods. *Breeding:* little known, but the fry have external gills at first.

Long-nosed Elephant Fish *Gnathonemus petersi* 250 mm 10 in. Africa, Cameroon: dark, turbid waters. Fishes in the Mormyridae family often have the lower lip extended into a finger-like digging tool. They also have electricity-generating cells that radiate a magnetic field around the fish, which assists navigation in the darkness. Nocturnal. *Temperature:* 24°C (75°F). *Diet:* worms and insect larvae, which should be provided in sufficient quantities to distend the stomach. *Breeding:* not yet bred in the aquarium.

Knife Fish; Featherback *Notopterus chitala* 710 mm 28½ in. Burma, Malaya, Thailand: various waters. This seemingly finless fish swims with a continuous, undulating movement of the long anal fin, which fringes almost the whole length of the body. Like *Gnathonemus petersi*, it is nocturnal and navigates in the darkness in a similar fashion. *Temperature:* 24°C (75°F). *Diet:* live foods preferred, but can be weaned on to dried foods. *Breeding:* eggs are deposited on rocks, and guarded by the male.

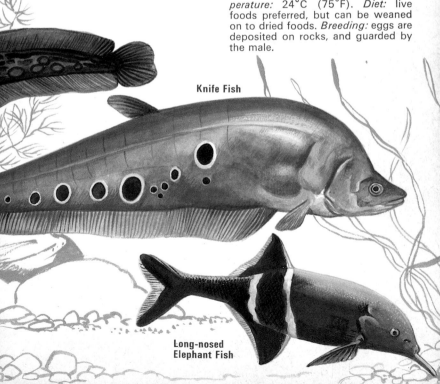

Knife Fish

Long-nosed Elephant Fish

BRACKISH WATER FISHES

These fishes are found in coastal waters and, although they may be kept in fresh water, generally thrive better in water to which an amount of sea-salt has been added. The usual amount is roughly 1-2 tablespoonsful per 10 litres (2 gallons).

Indian Glass Fish *Chanda ranga* (formerly *Ambassis lala*) 75 mm 3 in. India, Burma, Thailand. A delicately coloured, transparent fish, whose internal structure may be seen quite clearly. This member of the Centropomidae family is a shy fish, preferring a sunlit, but well-planted, tank. *Temperature:* 19-24°C (66-75°F). *Diet:* live foods. *Breeding:* eggs laid among plants; fry need tiny live food.

Bumble-bee Fish; Golden Banded Goby *Brachygobius xanthozona* 50 mm 2 in. Borneo, Java, Sumatra. This small fish can be quite possessive over its territory, and members of the Gobiidae family should be provided with rocky hiding places in the aquarium. *Temperature:* 20-25°C (68-76°F). *Diet:* live foods, particularly worms. *Breeding:* eggs laid in caves or flowerpots. The male guards.

Knight Goby *Stigmatogobius sadanundio* 90 mm 3½ in. Sunda Islands (Indonesia), Philippines. A very attractively marked fish, similar in patterning to some Killifishes. May take to completely fresh water more successfully than other brackish water species. *Temperature:* 21-24°C (70-75°F). *Diet:* worms, insect larvae. *Breeding:* not yet bred in the aquarium.

Mono; Malayan Angel; Fingerfish *Monodactylus argenteus* 150 mm 6 in. Indian Ocean coastal waters. Members of the Monodactylidae family resemble the fresh water Angel Fish in shape and colour, but they do not have the long, trailing fins. A taller species, *M. sebae,* has more black stripes. Monos appreciate plenty of swimming space and, despite being a shoaling fish, are easily frightened. *Temperature:* 24-28°C (75-82°F). *Diet:* all foods, particularly vegetable matter. *Breeding:* not yet bred in the aquarium.

Scat; Argus Fish *Scatophagus, argus* 250 mm 10 in. East Africa South and South-east Asia, Northern Australia. The family name Scatophagidae means 'dung-eaters', and this fish is often referred to as 'The Poor Man's Discus'. Like *Monodactylus argenteus,* a shoaling, but easily frightened fish. *Temperature:* 20-28°C (68-82°F). *Diet:* live and vegetable foods. This fish will eat aquarium plants. *Breeding:* not yet bred in the aquarium.

Indian Glass Fish

Bumble-bee Fish

Knight Goby

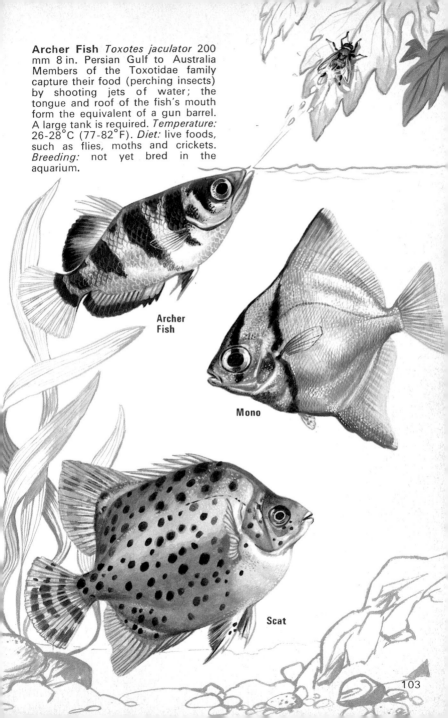

Archer Fish *Toxotes jaculator* 200 mm 8 in. Persian Gulf to Australia Members of the Toxotidae family capture their food (perching insects) by shooting jets of water; the tongue and roof of the fish's mouth form the equivalent of a gun barrel. A large tank is required. *Temperature:* 26-28°C (77-82°F). *Diet:* live foods, such as flies, moths and crickets. *Breeding:* not yet bred in the aquarium.

Archer
Fish

Mono

Scat

MARINE FISHES

Most of the brilliantly coloured, tropical marine fishes are native to the coral reefs of the Indo-Pacific oceans, and to some extent to the Red Sea. Because it would be impracticable to give exact natural locations, maps showing the distribution of genera have been omitted. Although the species described are tropical fishes, it is quite feasible (and rewarding) to keep species from cooler seas in the coldwater marine aquarium. Many species of *Blennius*, for example, together with invertebrate life from the same habitat, can provide an extra facet to fishkeeping without too much financial outlay. A day's outing to the coast can usefully be partly spent collecting local species of fishes or even seawater for the aquarium.

Marine fishkeeping is a relatively young branch of the hobby and has yet to become as fully documented as its freshwater counterpart; many of the fishes kept are, for want of further detailed information, given the same aquarium conditions in terms of temperature and food. Unless stated otherwise, all species of marine fishes described in the following pages are kept within the temperature range 24-26°C (75-79°F) and fed with a varied diet of live foods, fresh meat and sea-foods (shellfish), or suitably formulated flake foods.

A Red Sea Clownfish (Amphiprion bicinctus) safely at home.

ANEMONEFISHES AND CLOWNFISHES/ FAMILY AMPHIPRIONIDAE

In their natural habitat the Clownfishes share a fascinating relationship with the Sea-anemone (*Stoichactis*, *Discosoma* and *Radianthus* species). Normally, any fish venturing into the outspread tentacles of the Sea-anemone is fatally stung and consumed, but the Clownfish enjoys immunity (and safety from other larger fishes) as it swims in and out of its host. It is assumed that in return for this favour, the Sea-anemone receives scraps of food dropped by the tenant Clownfish. Clownfishes should therefore be kept with Sea-anemones in the aquarium wherever possible.

Tomato Clown; Fire Clown *Amphiprion ephippium* 120 mm 4¾ in. Indo-Pacific oceans. The body and fins are tomato red. A blurred dark oval patch appears on the flanks, and the gill covers may be similarly marked. A white stripe runs vertically across the head, although according to some sources this stripe should be missing; a fish fitting this description is *A. rubrocinctus.* Other sources indicate that the white stripe fades with age. Like all Clownfishes, this is a very territorially minded fish and is intolerant of its own species. *Temperature and diet:* see page 104. *Breeding:* some species of *Amphiprion* have spawned in the aquarium, but no fry yet raised.

Common Clown; Clown Anemonefish; Percula Clown *Amphiprion percula* 80 mm 3¼ in. Indo-Pacific oceans. Perhaps one of the best-known marine aquarium fishes. The patterns of red/orange, black and white appear to be hand-painted. Some importations of *A. percula* may in fact be *A. ocellaris,* which has less black in the markings than the true species. If a large enough Sea-anemone is available, more than one Clownfish can take up residence without too much squabbling. *Temperature and diet:* see page 104. *Breeding:* some species of *Amphiprion* have spawned in the aquarium.

Maroon Clownfish; Spine-cheeked Clownfish; Premnas *Premnas biaculeatus* 150 mm 6 in. Indo-Pacific oceans. This close relative of the Clownfishes has a deep red/brown, or maroon-coloured body crossed by three narrow white bands. One or two backward pointing spines are present below the eyes. This fish is aggressive towards Clownfishes and seems able to do without the company of a Sea-anemone. *Temperature* and *diet:* see page 104. *Breeding:* no details available.

Tomato
Clown

Common
Clown

Maroon
Clownfish

DAMSELFISHES AND SERGEANT-MAJORS/ FAMILY POMACENTRIDAE

Although related to the Clownfishes, these fishes have larger scales, and whereas the Clownfishes seek the relative safety of the Sea-anemone, the Damselfishes and Sergeant-Majors prefer to seek protection among the many coral branches of the reefs where they live. Some species have spawned in the aquarium.

Yellow-backed Damsel; Black-footed Sergeant-Major; Bow-tie Damsel; Blue Fin Damsel *Abudefduf melanopus* 70 mm 2¾ in. Indo-Pacific oceans. Also known as *Paraglyphidodon melanopus.* The bright yellow of the back and dorsal fin contrasts sharply with the grey/turquoise of the body and the black-edged turquoise ventral and anal fins. The caudal fin has yellow top and bottom edges. The eyes are yellow and turquoise, having half the eye in each coloured area of the body. Not too aggressive, but may be less hardy than other Damselfishes. *Temperature and diet:* see page 104. *Breeding:* no information available.

Yellow-tailed Blue Damsel; Saffron Blue Damsel *Abudefduf parasema* (formerly *Pomacentrus melanochir*) 100 mm 4 in. Indo-Pacific oceans. The blue body and yellow tail become less contrasting with age as the colours lose their original intensity. There are several similarly coloured fishes in the Pomacentridae group. This species may dig in the gravel, and the under-gravel filter should be protected by a mesh in the gravel (see *Pelvicachromis pulcher,* page 97). A hardy species, and not so aggressive as other Damselfishes. *Temperature and diet:* see page 104. *Breeding:* no information available.

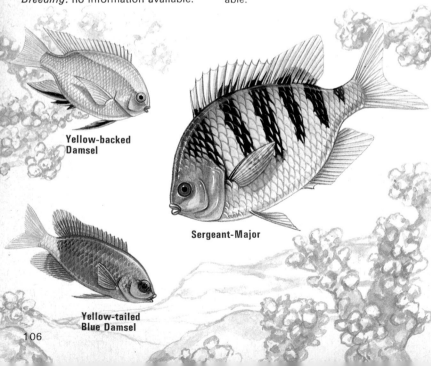

Yellow-backed Damsel

Sergeant-Major

Yellow-tailed Blue Damsel

Blue Puller

Humbug Damsel

Domino Damsel

Sergeant-Major *Abudefduf saxatilis* 180 mm 7 in. Indo-Pacific oceans. The silvery-blue body has a hint of yellow on the dorsal surface, and is crossed by six dark, vertical bands. A hardy fish, but may prove too aggressive when adult. Often a leader in the dash for food, and can be relied upon to teach shy fishes, which soon learn to follow its example. *Temperature and diet:* see page 104. *Breeding:* no information available.

Blue Puller *Chromis coeruleus* 130 mm 5 in. Indo-Pacific oceans, Red Sea. A uniformly coloured blue-green fish. The dorsal fin has hard and soft rays, and the caudal fin is deeply forked. A shoaling fish which should not be kept in isolation. This fish is rather susceptible to skin infections. *Temperature and diet:* see page 104. *Breeding:* has been spawned in the aquarium.

Humbug Damsel; Black and White Damsel; White-tailed Damsel or Humbug *Dascyllus aruanus* 80 mm 4¼ in. Indo-Pacific oceans, Red Sea. The body is silver-white and crossed by black bands, two of which slant backwards, the third being vertical. The dorsal and anal fins are black with white rear edges; the ventral fins are black; the caudal fin is white; the pectoral fins are clear. A shoaling fish which often 'adopts' a particular piece of coral or rock. Hardy, but aggressive towards other species. *Temperature and diet:* see page 104. *Breeding:* has spawned in the aquarium, but the fry not raised.

Domino Damsel; Three Spot Damsel *Dascyllus trimaculatus* 120 mm 4¾ in. Indo-Pacific oceans, Red Sea. An all-black fish, except for a white blotch on each flank and on the forehead. The intense black colour may fade with age. Hardy, but aggressive. *Temperature and diet:* see page 104. *Breeding:* only occasionally spawned in the aquarium.

107

BUTTERFLYFISHES AND ANGELFISHES/ FAMILY CHAETODONTIDAE

Members of this family are deep-bodied and laterally compressed fishes. They are found mainly in the Indo-Pacific oceans, but one or two species occur in the Atlantic. They inhabit coral reefs, constantly pecking or scraping food from the surface and crevices of the coral heads. Their brilliant colours and startling patterns may be either a type of camouflage in the brightly lit world of the coral reef, or an aid in recognizing or communicating with fishes of the same species. The Angelfishes are distinguished from the Butterflyfishes by a spine at the bottom rear corner of the gill cover; many young Angelfishes have colours and markings that differ from those of the adult form. Angelfishes are territorial, and fishes of the same species will fight.

Threadfin Butterflyfish *Chaetodon (Anisochaetodon) auriga* 200 mm 8 in, or slightly larger. Indo-Pacific oceans, Red Sea. Although the Butterflyfishes have a wide range of colour patterns, not many have a filamentous extension to the dorsal fin, which in this species also carries an 'eye-spot'. The function of the 'eye-spot' is to distract the attention of a predator from the real eye; for the same reason, the eyes of many species are hidden by a dark stripe. This fish is peaceful, but all Butterflyfishes appreciate a place to retreat to at night. They are shy feeders and may choose to starve rather than compete for food against more boisterous fishes in the tank. *Temperature and diet:* see page 104. *Breeding:* no information available.

Pakistani Butterfly; Collared Coralfish *Chaetodon collare* 150 mm 6 in. Indo-Pacific oceans. The vulnerable eye is well-disguised in this species. A dark lattice-work pattern covers most of the body. This species is considered to be more difficult to keep than other Butterflyfishes. *Temperature and diet:* see page 104. *Breeding:* no information available.

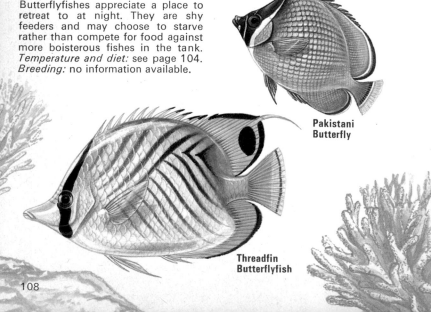

Pakistani
Butterfly

Threadfin
Butterflyfish

Copper-banded Butterflyfish; Beaked Coralfish; Long-nosed Butterflyfish *Chelmon rostratus* 170 mm 7 in. Indo-Pacific oceans, Red Sea. The extended 'nose' of this fish is actually its mouth, and is ideally suited to picking out food from deep crevices in the coral reef. A temperamental feeder, often in reaction to changes in the water chemistry (which should be checked immediately), and aggressive towards its own species. *Temperature and diet:* see page 104. *Breeding:* no information available.

Long-snouted Coralfish; Forceps Fish *Forcipiger longirostris* 180 mm 7½ in, or slightly larger. Indo-Pacific oceans, Red Sea. The body shape is almost identical to that of *Chelmon rostratus,* but the coloration is entirely different. However, this fish does share the same characteristic of being a fussy feeder (although it is not so aggressive) and is not a fish for the newcomer to marine fish-keeping. *Temperature and diet:* see page 104. *Breeding:* no information available.

Wimple Fish; Pennant Coralfish; Poor Man's Moorish Idol; Featherfin Bullfish *Heniochus acumineatus* 200 mm 8 in. Indo-Pacific oceans, Red Sea. The sloping black stripes on the white body give the fish a leaning forward appearance, but the main physical feature is the long, banner-like dorsal fin. Easy to keep, becoming quite tame. Young specimens often act like Cleanerfishes (see *Labroides dimidiatus,* page 115). This fish is often confused with the Moorish Idol (*Zanclus canescens,* page 113), but lacks its spines and horns. *Temperature and diet:* see page 104. *Breeding:* no information available.

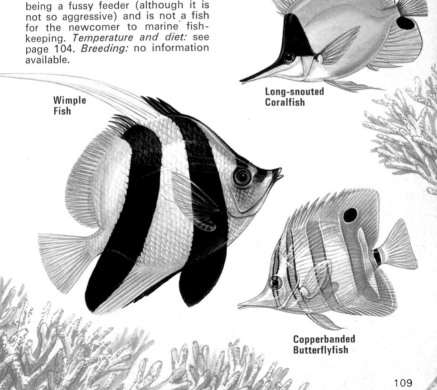

Long-snouted Coralfish

Wimple Fish

Copperbanded Butterflyfish

Black and Gold Angelfish; Oriole Angelfish; Two-coloured Angelfish; Bicolor Cherub *Centropyge bicolor* 100 mm 4 in. Pacific Ocean. A popular fish, which does not grow too large, and is not so territorially minded as other Angelfishes. It may be necessary to experiment a little to persuade this fish to feed readily; it should be started on live Brine Shrimp and gradually offered more convenient, and larger, foods such as frozen shrimp. *Temperature and diet:* see page 104. *Breeding:* no information available.

Rock Beauty *Holacanthus tricolor* 610 mm 24½ in. Caribbean. The young fish is yellow with a blue-edged dark spot on each flank. With adulthood the spot broadens into a large dark patch. The eyes have bright blue segments. The anal and dorsal fins are edged with red. The fish's size demands that it be given a large tank, and it may bully other fishes if kept in too small an aquarium. *Temperature and diet:* see page 104. However, the diet should also include vegetable matter such as algae, spinach or lettuce. *Breeding:* no information available.

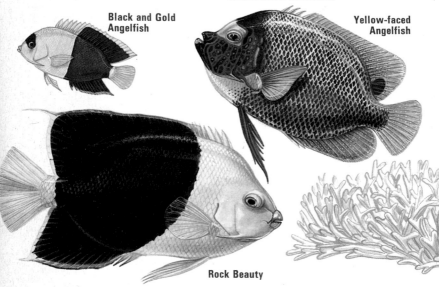

Black and Gold Angelfish

Yellow-faced Angelfish

Rock Beauty

Yellow-faced Angelfish; Blue-faced Angelfish *Euxiphipops xanthometapon* 460 mm 18½ in. Indo-Pacific oceans. Another fish that may take a little time to settle down to aquarium life and may be a fussy feeder. Providing all the conditions, such as water composition and temperature, are satisfactory and the feeding hurdle has been overcome, the fish usually does well in the aquarium. *Temperature and diet:* see page 104. However, the diet should also include some vegetable matter. *Breeding:* no information available.

Blue Ring Angelfish *Pomacanthus annularis* 400 mm 16 in. Indo-Pacific oceans. The blue ring on the forward part of the brown, blue-lined body is the identifying mark of this species. The juvenile fish has many vertical, light-coloured bands and a yellow, transverse bands across the gills. The blue facial markings fade with age, and the only common characteristic between young and adult fishes is the yellow/orange caudal fin. *Temperature and diet:* see page 104. However, vegetable matter is also required. *Breeding:* no information available.

Black or **Grey Angelfish** *Pomacanthus arcuatus* 450 mm 18 in. Atlantic Ocean, Caribbean. The young fish is black with six vertical, bright yellow bands crossing the body and fins. The adult fish is grey with one or two faint, white vertical bands, and a white mouth. The juvenile fish is often confused with the similarly marked young *P. paru*, whose yellow bands continue right across the fins instead of stopping midway, as in *P. arcuatus*. *Temperature and diet:* see page 104. However, some vegetable matter should be given. *Breeding:* no information available.

Blue Ring Angelfish

Black Angelfish

Imperial Angelfish

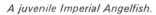

A juvenile Imperial Angelfish.

Imperial or **Emperor Angelfish** *Pomacanthus imperator* 400 mm 16 in. Indo-Pacific oceans, Red Sea. The juvenile fish is blue with a concentric pattern of white lines, and is very similar to the juvenile forms of *P. annularis* and *P. semicirculatus*. This fish requires a clean aquarium, and the water should be partially changed regularly. *Temperature and diet:* see page 104. However, vegetable matter should be given. *Breeding:* no information available.

111

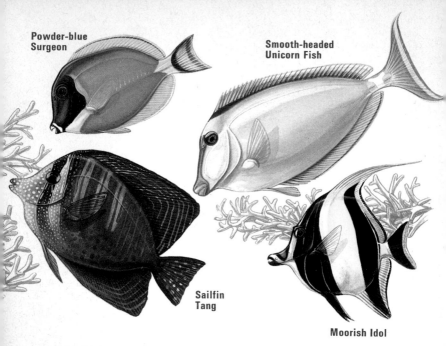

Powder-blue Surgeon

Smooth-headed Unicorn Fish

Sailfin Tang

Moorish Idol

SURGEONS, TANGS AND UNICORNFISHES/ FAMILY ACANTHURIDAE

These brightly coloured, oval-bodied fishes have sharp, bony scalpels on the caudal peduncle which can cause painful wounds. Some species have fixed scalpels, others a protruding horn above the eyes.

Powder-blue Surgeon *Acanthurus leucosternon* 300 mm 12 in. Indo-Pacific oceans. The delicate blue of the body contrasts with the black face and yellow dorsal fin. The retracted scalpel on each side of the yellow caudal peduncle can be clearly seen. A fish for the experienced marine fishkeeper, requiring plenty of swimming space and a vigorously aerated aquarium. *Temperature and diet:* see page 104. However, some vegetable food should also be provided. *Breeding:* no information available.

Smooth-headed Unicorn Fish; Japanese Tang *Naso lituratus* 500 mm 20 in. Indo-Pacific oceans. This fish's colour pattern gives its face a definite expression. The two fixed spines on each side of the caudal peduncle are set in bright orange patches. The outside rays of the caudal fin are pronounced. *Temperature and Diet:* see page 104. However, vegetable foods should also be given. *Breeding:* no information available.

Sailfin Tang *Zebrasoma veliferum* 400 mm 16 in. Indo-Pacific oceans. The large, rounded dorsal and anal fins give an outline similar to that of the freshwater Discus (*Symphysodon*), and the body markings are also similar. The body shape is not disc-like but has the pointed, oval form normal to the Surgeonfish family. It is a hardy fish and may well become tame, accepting food from the hand. *Temperature and diet:* see page 104. However, vegetable foods should occasionally be included. *Breeding:* no information available.

MOORISH IDOL/ FAMILY ZANCLIDAE

Although there is only one species in the family, it is very widespread throughout the Indo-Pacific oceans. It is similar to the *Heniochus* species in the Family Chaetodontidae but is more closely related to the Acanthuridae.

Moorish Idol; Toby *Zanclus canescens* 230 mm 9½ in. Indo-Pacific oceans. The dorsal fin of this fish often extends into a long banner-like streamer. Juvenile fishes have sharp spines at the corner of the mouth, and adults have horns in front of the eyes. The common name refers to the reverence with which some Moslem communities regard this fish. It requires a large aquarium with a good growth of algae from which, hopefully, the fish will pick its food. It may, however, be reluctant to feed, and is not a beginner's fish. *Temperature and diet:* see page 104. However, some vegetable matter is needed. *Breeding:* no information available.

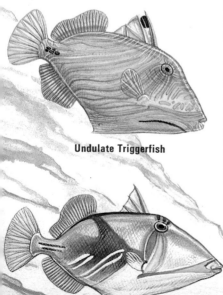

Undulate Triggerfish

TRIGGERFISHES/ FAMILY BALISTIDAE

These fishes have two dorsal fins, the first of which consists of only three spines; the first spine is erectile and can be locked into position by the second spine. The first dorsal fin is usually held flat, but is erected when danger threatens. It is often used to secure the fish in a crevice, thus preventing capture. Another unusual feature is the absence of ventral fins.

Undulate Triggerfish; Orange-green Triggerfish *Balistapus undulatus* 350 mm 14 in. Indo-Pacific oceans. This fish exhibits another peculiar family characteristic — that of resting head-down or lying on its side, much to the alarm of its owner. Triggerfishes have strong jaws and teeth, making the keeping of invertebrates in the same tank impracticable; they should be fed whole shellfish and small crabs to help keep their teeth worn down. Not a fussy feeder, but aggressive. *Temperature and diet:* see page 104. *Breeding:* the fish may burrow into the sand and deposit eggs in the depression; the eggs are guarded.

Picasso Trigger; White-barred Triggerfish *Rhinecanthus aculeatus* 300 mm 12 in. Indo-Pacific oceans. The abstract-art markings of this fish are the obvious inspiration for its common name, and perhaps the exaggerated mouth markings help to deter predators. The sharp teeth necessitate caution when handling. Feeding is no particular problem, but the fish may be aggressive when adult. *Temperature and diet:* see page 104. *Breeding:* no information available.

Picasso Trigger

WRASSES AND HOGFISHES/ FAMILY LABRIDAE

The Wrasses are found in all tropical seas. Like the Angelfishes, they display a wide difference in colour patterns between juvenile and adult fishes. Some Wrasses perform a cleaning service by removing skin parasites from other fishes. In nature, fishes often visit the Cleaner Wrasses' reef deliberately to avail themselves of this service. Wrasses often lie on the aquarium floor to rest at night, or bury themselves in the sand; others spin a mucous sleeping bag which is discarded each morning.

Cuban Hogfish *Bodianus pulchellus* 230 mm 9 in. Caribbean. This fish is not difficult to feed, accepting shellfish meat, algae and, after a little training, flake food. Swimming is effected by the pectoral fins only, the caudal fin being used for steering only. Although the mouth is small, this fish will eagerly snap up other small fishes. *Temperature and diet:* see page 104. *Breeding:* some species of the Labridae group have spawned, but the fry have not survived.

Clown Labrid; Twinspot Wrasse *Coris angulata* 1220 mm 48 in. Indo-Pacific oceans. Unfortunately, the young fish soon matures and loses its colour patterns when about 100 mm long. The adult fish is green, and has yellow and purple edges to the dorsal and anal fins. Because it grows quickly, this fish is not suitable for the aquarium for very long. Other smaller species such as *C. gaimardi gaimardi*, *C. gaimardi africana* and *C. formosa* do not grow so fast, and the juvenile forms are also brightly coloured. *Temperature and diet:* see page 104. *Breeding:* no information available.

Bird Wrasse *Gomphosus coeruleus* 270 mm 11 in. Indo-Pacific coastal waters. The adult male is cobalt blue or green with green fins, but females and young males are brownish with brown or reddish spotted scales, and some red colour on the snout. The elongated snout is an excellent tool for picking out food from crevices in rocks and coral. The names *G. varius* and *G. tricolor* are sometimes seen, but may have been wrongly conferred on young specimens of *G. coeruleus*. *Temperature and diet:* see page 104. Also requires algae. *Breeding:* no information available.

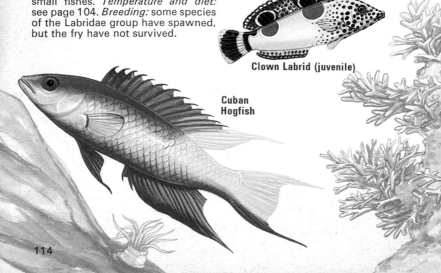

Clown Labrid (juvenile)

Cuban Hogfish

Cleaner Wrasse; Cleaner Labrid
Labroides dimidiatus 100 mm 4 in.
Indo-Pacific oceans. This fish has
both female and male organs and if a
dominant male in a group dies, a
female fish will develop into a male
to take its place. This cleaning fish
has its imitators, the most notable
being *Aspidontus tractus* (page 119).
(These other imitators make use of
their mimicry talents to approach
other fishes for quite a different
purpose, often leaving with a piece
of flesh torn from the unsuspecting
victim). *L. dimidiatus* may be clearly
recognized by its terminal mouth,
whereas the mouth of *A. tractus* is
underslung. *Temperature and diet:*
see page 104. Despite its constant
attention to other fishes, this fish
cannot sustain itself totally on
parasites picked from the skin of
other fishes, and its diet must be
supplemented with finely chopped
meaty foods and crumbled flake
foods. *Breeding:* no information
available.

Green Wrasse; Moon Wrasse
Thalassoma lunare 300 mm 12 in.
Indo-Pacific oceans. A beautiful fish
that is constantly on the move
(seemingly effortlessly so), being
propelled only by the pectoral fins.
A hardy fish and not a fussy feeder.
It often buries itself in the sand at
night. The caudal fin is crescent-
shaped and the markings on the
pectoral fins distinguish this fish
from the very similar, but smaller,
T. lutescens. A fairly peaceful fish,
but it may worry smaller fishes.
Temperature and diet: see page 104.
Breeding: no information available.

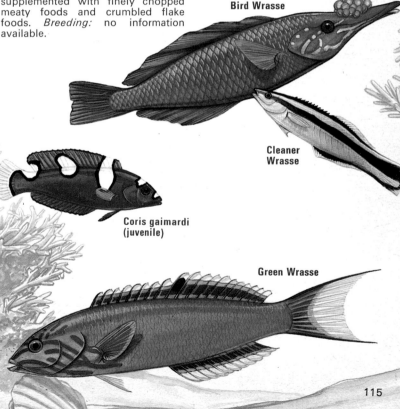

Bird Wrasse

Cleaner
Wrasse

Coris gaimardi
(juvenile)

Green Wrasse

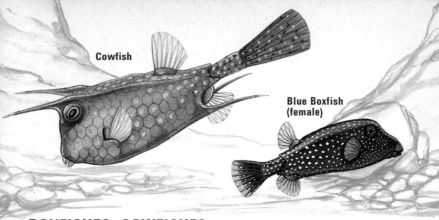

Cowfish

Blue Boxfish
(female)

BOXFISHES, COWFISHES AND TRUNKFISHES/ FAMILY OSTRACIIDAE

These strange fishes have bony plates covering the body instead of scales; the body is box-shaped and without ventral fins. Their flesh is reportedly poisonous, and some species release toxic substances when dead or when frightened (this often kills the Boxfish too in the confines of the aquarium). They are generally bottom feeders.

Blue Boxfish *Ostracion lentiginosum* 200 mm 8 in. Indo-Pacific oceans. The female fish is as illustrated but the male fish may also have a red coloration. When frightened, Boxfishes often fold their caudal fin forward along the side of the body. They may be susceptible to skin infections. *Temperature and diet:* see page 104. Brine Shrimp is often used to accustom Boxfishes to aquarium foods. *Breeding:* no information available.

Cowfish *Lactoria cornuta* 500 mm 20 in. Indo-Pacific oceans. An easily recognized species with two cowlike horns which project forward from the head; two other spines extend from the rear part of the body. *Temperature and diet:* see page 104, but small live foods preferred. *Breeding:* lays floating eggs.

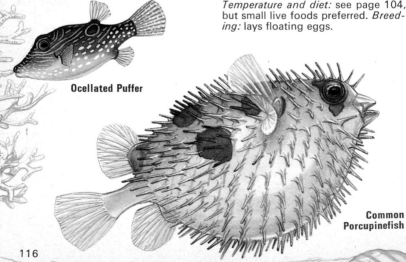

Ocellated Puffer

Common Porcupinefish

MISCELLANEOUS SPECIES

Ocellated Puffer; Peacock-eyed Sharp-nosed Puffer *Canthigaster margaritatus* 150 mm 6 in. Indo-Pacific oceans. A member of the Sharp-nosed Puffer family (Canthigasteridae), which defend themselves by inflating their bodies into ball shapes with air or water. This species, which is also known as *C. marginatus, C. papua* and *C. solandri,* settles down well in the aquarium. But it may be aggressive towards its own species and also nip the long fins of other fishes. When taken from the water it may emit croacking noises. *Temperature and diet:* see page 104. *Breeding:* no information available.

Common Porcupinefish *Diodon hystrix* 900 mm 36 in. All warm seas, including some temperate areas. This large fish is the commonest of the Porcupinefishes (Family Diodontidae), which defend themselves with sharp spines as well as by inflating themselves. However, this species cannot always deflate itself easily and is often washed ashore in the inflated condition. *Temperature and diet:* see page 104. This fish prefers animal food and crushed snails from freshwater tanks. It should not be kept with smaller fishes. *Breeding:* no information available.

Panther Fish; Polka Dot Grouper; Barramundi Cod *Cromileptes altivelis* 500 mm 20 in. Indo-Pacific oceans. A beautiful representative of the Serranidae family, comprising Rock Cods and Groupers, which are large predatory fishes without ventral fins. The white body and fins of this species are speckled with large black dots. It is a very hardy fish, but should only be kept with fishes of its own size. *Temperature and diet:* see page 104. *Breeding:* no information available.

Royal Gramma; Fairy Basslet *Gramma loreto* 80 mm 3 in. Caribbean. A startlingly coloured fish which spends most of its time in caves and other hiding places. It is a member of the Basslet family (Grammidae), which are similar to, but less aggressive than, the Serranidae group. Because this fish is a good jumper the aquarium should be covered at all times. A similar species is the False Gramma, or Royal Dottyback (*Pseudochromis paccagnella*), whose identical colours are separated by a narrow white band. *Temperature and diet:* see page 104. *Breeding:* the male builds a nest of algae and small pieces of coral. Eggs have been observed in the aquarium, but no fry have been raised.

Royal
Gramma

Panther
Fish

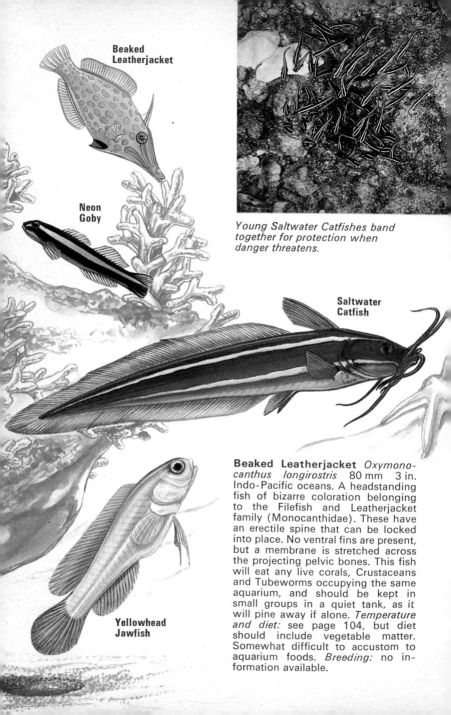

Beaked Leatherjacket

Neon Goby

Young Saltwater Catfishes band together for protection when danger threatens.

Saltwater Catfish

Yellowhead Jawfish

Beaked Leatherjacket *Oxymono-canthus longirostris* 80 mm 3 in. Indo-Pacific oceans. A headstanding fish of bizarre coloration belonging to the Filefish and Leatherjacket family (Monocanthidae). These have an erectile spine that can be locked into place. No ventral fins are present, but a membrane is stretched across the projecting pelvic bones. This fish will eat any live corals, Crustaceans and Tubeworms occupying the same aquarium, and should be kept in small groups in a quiet tank, as it will pine away if alone. *Temperature and diet:* see page 104, but diet should include vegetable matter. Somewhat difficult to accustom to aquarium foods. *Breeding:* no information available.

Yellowhead Jawfish *Opistognathus aurifrons* 120 mm 5 in. Caribbean. Jawfishes and Smilers (Family Opisthognathidae) are bottom-dwelling fishes that retreat, tail first, into burrows when threatened. The delicate blue body of this species is often hidden in the aquarium gravel, with only the rather sad-expressioned yellow head visible. *Temperature and diet:* see page 104. However, small live foods should also be given. *Breeding:* a mouthbrooder, but no fry have been raised in the aquarium.

False Cleaner *Aspidontus tractus* 100 mm 4 in. Indo-Pacific oceans. A member of the Blenny family (Blenniidae), which are found in all tidal waters and rock pools. This species is the closest imitator of the Cleaner Wrasse (*Labroides dimidiatus,* page 115), but can be distinguished by its underslung mouth. The False Cleaner uses its disguise to approach close enough to tear off a lump of flesh from its unsuspecting victim. It is best kept with its own kind in an aquarium with plenty of retreats. *Temperature and diet:* see page 104. *Breeding:* no information available.

False Cleaner

Mandarin Fish

Saltwater Catfish; Striped Catfish; Coral Catfish; Barber *Plotosus anguillaris* 900 mm 36 in. Indo-Pacific oceans. The young of the shoaling saltwater Catfishes (Family Plotosidae) gather together in a tight ball with their heads outwards when frightened. This smartly marked species grows very fast, and the markings disappear with age. The spines are poisonous, and the fish should be handled with care. *Temperature and diet:* see page 104. *Breeding:* no information available.

Neon Goby *Elactinus oceanops* 60 mm 2½ in. Caribbean. Like their freshwater relations, the saltwater Gobies (Family Gobiidae) spend most of their time scurrying around the aquarium floor. The Neon Goby is similar in body shape and markings to the Cleaner Wrasse (*Labroides dimidiatus,* page 115), and it performs a limited cleaning service for other fishes in the aquarium. *Temperature and diet:* see page 104. *Breeding:* has been spawned in the aquarium. Adults guard the eggs and young.

Mandarin Fish *Synchiropus splendidus* 70 mm 3 in. Indo-Pacific oceans. Mandarin Fishes and Dragonets (Family Callionymidae) inhabit tidal rock pools. This species, like many other males of the family, has an elongated first dorsal fin. Its common name derives from the oriental-looking colour patterns on the body. It seems to do best if kept on its own, but is difficult to acclimatize to aquarium foods. *Temperature and diet:* see page 104. *Breeding:* no information available.

Lionfish; Dragonfish; Turkeyfish
Pterois volitans 350 mm 14 in. Indo-Pacific oceans, Red Sea. The Lionfish and Scorpionfish family (Scorpaenidae) have poisonous spines. Their coloration and waving fin rays disguise them ideally as they lie in wait for their prey. This species is a favourite exhibit at public aquaria, but it may prove to have too healthy an appetite for the home aquarium. A similar species, P. *radiata,* has more red in its coloration, even longer fin rays, but fewer white markings. *Temperature and diet:* see page 104. However, this fish needs large quantities of live, moving foods, such as Goldfish. *Breeding:* no information available.

Pyjama Cardinalfish; Polka Dot Cardinalfish *Sphaeramia* (*Apogon*) *nematopterus* 100 mm 4 in. Indo-Pacific oceans. Members of the Cardinalfish family (Apogonidae) have double dorsal fins, are nocturnal by nature, and tend to remain stationary for long periods. This species is a curiously patterned fish, which appears to be made up of parts from very different fishes. *Temperature and diet:* see page 104. However, live foods are preferred. *Breeding:* a mouthbrooder, but no specific information available.

Spotted Sea-horse; Golden Sea-horse *Hippocampus kuda* 300 mm 12 in, smaller in the aquarium. Indo-Pacific oceans. This fish, which everyone knows and wants to keep in the aquarium, belongs to the Sea-horse and Pipefish family (Syngnathidae). It swims in a vertical or forward-slanting position, and anchors itself to branches of coral or a Sea Fan. Other species of Sea-horses include *H. hudsonius* and *H. zosterae,* both Atlantic Ocean species. *Temperature and diet:* see page 104. However, small live foods are essential, even young freshwater Guppy fry. *Breeding:* the male fish incubates fertilized eggs in its abdominal pouch.

Red Squirrelfish *Holocentrus ruber* 230 mm 9 in. Indo-Pacific oceans, Red Sea. The Holocentridae family, comprising Squirrelfishes and Soldierfishes, are predatory, nocturnal fishes which hide in crevices during the daytime. In this species, the usual red coloration of the family is broken by lighter-coloured horizontal bands. The large eyes indicate the fish's nocturnal nature. *Temperature and diet:* see page 104. *Breeding:* some species of Holocentridae have been seen to spawn in the aquarium.

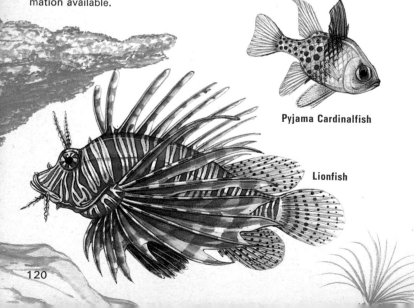

Pyjama Cardinalfish

Lionfish

Fox-face; Foxfish Lo (*Siganus*) *vulpinus* 250 mm 10 in. Pacific Ocean. A member of the Spinefeet and Rabbitfish family (Siganidae), which are similar in shape to the Surgeonfishes (Family Acanthuridae, see page 112), but have no scalpels on the caudal peduncle. They normally swim head-downwards, and most of the family are herbivorous. This species is the exception in the family in possessing a tubular snout with a terminal mouth. The spines of its dorsal fin are poisonous. *Temperature and diet:* see page 104. However, vegetable matter should also be provided. *Breeding:* no information available.

Round Batfish *Platax orbicularis* 500 mm 20 in. Indo-Pacific oceans. Members of the Batfish family (Platacidae) are characterized by their disc-shaped bodies, while the juvenile forms also have extremely elongated fins. It is believed that Batfishes can release a poisonous mucus into the water as a defence mechanism. Some confusion surrounds the exact number of species; some sources treat *P. orbicularis* and *P. teira* as synonyms for *P. pinnatus,* whereas others regard all three as separate species. Batfishes appreciate a tall, spacious tank, and young specimens soon outgrow the aquarium. Although they are peaceful and can become tame, they are easily frightened. *Temperature and diet:* see page 104. *Breeding:* no information available.

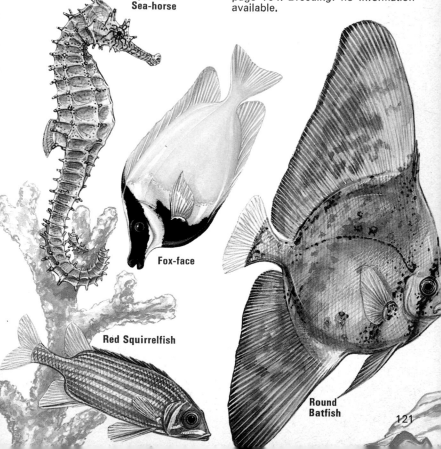

Spotted Sea-horse

Fox-face

Red Squirrelfish

Round Batfish

INDEX

Fishes (Scientific Names)

125